WORLD OF SOCCER:

A COMPLETE GUIDE TO THE WORLD'S MOST POPULAR SPORT

Ashley Jude Collie

This Library Edition First Published and Exclusively Distributed by
The Rosen Publishing Group, Inc.
New York

To my dad Ashley, Senior, a lifelong Red Devils fan, who took me to my first soccer game, an international match between Wales and England. The 30,000 fans singing the national anthem and the buzz (electricity) in the air made me a lifelong soccer fan. —Ashley Jude Collie

This library edition first published in 2003 and exclusively distributed by
The Rosen Publishing Group, Inc., New York

Book Design: Michelle Innes
Additional editorial material: Shira Laskin

Photo credits: Cover (left), pp. 15, 58 © Action Images/Icon SMI; cover (center), pp. 25, 72 © Icon Sports Media; cover (right), p. 8 © DPPI/Icon SMI; all background images © Photodisc; p. 29 © John McDonough/SI/Icon SMI; p. 31 © Isaac Menashe/Icon SMI; p. 41 © Gary Rothstein/Icon SMI; p. 45 © Gary Rothstein/Icon SMI; p. 52 © Isaac Menashe/Icon SMI; pp. 62, 64 © Bob Falcetti/Icon SMI; p. 77 courtesy of The University of the South

First Edition

Library of Congress Cataloging-in-Publication Data

Collie, Ashley Jude.
  World of soccer : a complete guide to the world's most popular sport /
Ashley Jude Collie.-- 1st ed.
      p. cm.
"Sports Illustrated for kids books."
Summary: Explores soccer in the United States and around the world, presenting brief biographies of current soccer stars, describing the major events and leagues, and explaining the rules of the game.
Includes bibliographical references (p.   ) and index.
  ISBN 0-8239-3698-8
  1. Soccer--Juvenile literature. [1. Soccer.] I. Title.
  GV943.25 .C655 2003
  796.334--dc21

                            2002006614

>> CONTENTS

>> INTRODUCTION

IN THE BEGINNING

People have been playing kickball games for more than 2,000 years. The ancient Chinese, Japanese, Greeks, and Romans used everything from stuffed animal skins and stomachs, to human skulls as balls.

Roman soldiers played a form of soccer to keep fit. They brought their game to England around the year A.D. 217. The English took up the sport with gusto. There were no formal rules. Whole towns played at one time, with as many as 500 players on each team!

Centuries rolled by, and soccer became more organized. In 1863, several teams in England created the Football Association (F.A.). The F.A. agreed upon a set of rules that became the basis for the modern game. English sailors introduced soccer to the countries they visited. By 1900, soccer was popular all over Europe and South America.

Today, soccer — or "football," as it's called in other countries — is the most popular sport on the planet. It is played or watched by billions of people. This book is your guide to the world of soccer. You'll meet the greatest stars of the past and the present, and read about the big events, leagues, records, and the rules of the game (see page 100) — the modern game, not the one played with skulls. We think you'll get a kick out of the *World of Soccer.*

>> THE WORLD CUP

What is the world's biggest sports event? The Super Bowl? The Olympics? The World Series?

Nope. It's soccer's World Cup Tournament.

Almost two billion people watched the men's final match that was played in Paris, France, in June 1998. An estimated 3.7 billion people around the world watched the whole month-long tournament on TV. Forty million TV viewers watched the 1999 Women's World Cup final.

The World Cup is soccer's ultimate championship. It is a wild, roaring spectacle of crazy, flag-waving fans with their faces painted in their national colors. The fans chant and sing and pound on drums as they cheer on their teams. A record total of 3.5 million fans attended the 52 games of the 1994 men's World Cup tournament, which was held in nine cities around the United States. That's an average crowd of almost 69,000 fans per game.

The World Cup is organized by Federation Internationale des Football Associations (FIFA), which governs soccer for men and women all over the world. The World Cup tournament for men was introduced in 1930.

The Women's World Cup was established in 1991. Both the men's and women's tournaments are held every four years in a different country. Teams are made up of a country's best players. Male and female soccer stars often play for pro teams in leagues in different countries, but they return to play for their national teams at World Cup time.

In 2000, men's teams from 195 countries began playing qualifying matches for the 2002 World Cup, which was held in Japan and South Korea. Teams were divided into six regions: Europe, South America, CONCACAF (North America, Central America and the Carribbean), Africa, Asia, and Oceania (Australia, New Zealand, Japan, and several small island nations). The 29 best teams from these six regions, plus the host nations (Japan and South Korea) and the defending World Cup champion (France), advanced to the tournament. It began on May 31, 2002.

The 32 countries that qualify form eight groups of four teams each (*see page 20*). Each group plays three games. The two teams with the best records from each group advance to the "Round of 16" where the winner of each game moves on to the next game. The loser goes home. The rounds continue until the final two teams battle for the world championship of soccer.

The Women's World Cup became popular in 1999 (*see page 21*).

LEGENDARY TEAM

The World Cup's greatest team ever may have been the awesome squad from Brazil that won the tournament in 1970. Pelé *(see page 15)* and his seemingly magical teammates loved to play to the beat of their fans' samba drums. Brazil's offense was overpowering, its defense was rock-solid, and the entire team played with breathtaking wizardry.

On offense, forward Jairzinho made World Cup history by scoring at least once in all six of Brazil's matches (for a total of seven goals). The defense, led by captain Carlos Alberto, often surprised opponents by attacking — and scoring.

The 1970 World Cup was held in Mexico. In a game for the Ages, Brazil beat defending World Cup champion England, 1–0, in early group play. Pelé and forward Tostao set up Jairzinho for the only goal of the game. Brazil went on to trounce Italy, 4–1, in the final game to win the Cup and the honor of being called the best team of all time.

MEN'S WORLD CUP

CURRENT STAR | RONALDO

Ronaldo probably has the most famous face in soccer. His shaved head and goofy, gap-toothed smile make him look like a big kid. That's only fitting, because he plays with a kid's joy.

Nicknamed "the Phenomenon," Brazil's superstar forward is a goal-scoring machine. He leaves the world's best defenders gasping for air as he dashes past them and blasts the ball into the net with either foot. Ronaldo scored a whopping 115 goals in only 148 games during his first five seasons in Europe's best pro leagues.

Ronaldo was born on September 22, 1976, in one of the poorest neighbor- hoods of Rio de Janeiro, Brazil's largest city. Growing up poor made him fiercely determined to succeed. Ronaldo boldly declared at age 13: "I will become the best in the world. I will be rich and help my family."

At age 15, Ronaldo joined a local pro club and scored 58 goals in 60 games. (Outside of the United States, teams often belong to organizations called "clubs.") At 17, he was a substitute on Brazil's national team that won the 1994 World Cup. That year, Ronaldo also played for a pro club in Holland, and was the country's top scorer with 35 goals.

Soccer experts around the world were beginning to notice Ronaldo. In 1996, he was sold for $19.2 million to the Spanish powerhouse team, Barcelona. He became an international superstar, scoring 34 goals in 37 league matches and winning the 1996 FIFA World Player of the Year award. He basked in the spotlight of the 1996 Summer Olympics, helping Brazil win the bronze medal. "Ronaldomania" was born.

In 1997, Ronaldo was sold again, to Inter Milan, in Italy. The price this time was $27 million! He scored 25 goals in 32 league games. His new teammates celebrated his goals by pretending to shine his shoes, they were so honored to have him as a teammate. At the age of 21, Ronaldo was named FIFA World Player of the Year for the second straight year. He had become the most famous soccer player in the world — the Michael Jordan of his sport.

FAST FACT

Soccer players from Brazil are often called by only one name, usually a nickname. It has been a Brazilian tradition for more than 50 years. Some of the most famous single names are Pelé, Ronaldo, and Romario. Players use one name because it is easier to say than their full names. Ronaldo's full name is Ronaldo Luiz Nazario de Lima. Make a cheer out of *that* name!

Many soccer fans expect Ronaldo to lead Brazil to a World Cup championship. The 1998 tournament was a disappointment for him and his many fans. Opponents concentrated on stopping him, and he was held to only four goals in seven games. He is now sharpening his skills by playing in Italy's toughest pro league: Serie A (*see page 85*).

STAR TO WATCH RIVALDO

Brazilian striker Rivaldo Victor Borba Ferreira is a master passer, playmaker, and free-kick taker. Rivaldo scored three goals, and set up two more to spark Brazil into the final World Cup game against France in 1998. He played for Barcelona of Spain's Primera Division in 1998–99 and scored 24 goals in 37 games. He was chosen the 1999 FIFA World Player of the Year.

Rivaldo suffered a severe left ankle injury in early 2002 and Brazil faced the possibility of preparing for the World Cup without him. He recovered, however, and was able to join his squad in the competition.

YOUNG STAR MICHAEL OWEN

Striker Michael Owen, of England, is a speed demon who burst upon the World Cup in 1998, when he was only 18 years old. He was the youngest player ever to compete for England's national team and the youngest to

FAST FACT

The World Cup trophy was stolen while it was on display in London, England, four months before the finals of the 1966 tournament. The culprit was an English dockworker. The trophy was found seven days later — wrapped in a newspaper and buried in a garden — by a dog named Pickles!

score a goal for England in the World Cup. Against Argentina, he took a pass, flashed like lightning through the defense, and fired a laser shot past the goalie. Many fans called it the best goal of the tournament. Such dazzling footwork is business-as-usual for Michael. He is a two-time co-winner of the Golden Boot award as the leading goal-scorer in England's highest league, the Premiership. He helped Liverpool sweep the FA Cup, League Cup, and UEFA Cup titles last season. He was named European Footballer of the Year in December 2001.

Michael faced knee, hamstring, and ankle injuries as England's national team began practicing for World Cup 2002. But he fired three goals for England against Germany in a 5–1 World Cup qualifier in September 2001.

FAST FACT

Wayne Gretzky made number 99 famous in hockey. Baseball retired number 42 in honor of Jackie Robinson. Soccer's most famous jersey number is 10. It was worn by the legendary Pelé, and is usually given to a team's striker. Strikers around the world consider it a great honor to wear Pelé's number 10, especially if they are from Brazil.

PAST STAR LOTHAR MATTHAUS

Lothar was a dynamo in midfield, with his thunderous shot, lightning speed, and aggressive defensive skills. He is the only field player who played in five World Cups. Lothar led Germany to the 1990 World Cup title. It was Germany's third World Cup win. He was the European and World Player of the Year in 1991.

In 1999, Lothar tied the world record for appearances on a men's national team (143). He starred in two top club leagues: Germany's Bundesliga [Bun-dis-LEE-ga] and Italy's Serie A.

Lothar played the 2000 season in Major League Soccer (MLS) for the New York/New Jersey MetroStars. He retired from active play at the end of the season.

GREATEST MOMENTS

TV broadcaster Andres Cantor became famous during the 1994 World Cup for screaming *"G-O-O-O-O-A-A-A-A-L!!!"* at the top of his lungs whenever a player fired a shot into the net. Andres is a broadcaster for Telemundo, a Spanish-language TV network.

PAST STAR DIEGO MARADONA

A tiny, powerful midfielder, Diego was only 5 feet 5 inches tall. But he fired cannon shots and juked his way past defenders with amazing ease. Diego played for Argentina in four World Cups, winning the 1986 cham–pionship and losing the final in 1990. At his peak, he was considered the greatest soccer player since Pelé.

Diego grew up poor. He began playing for top club teams in Argentina at age 16. He then left his country in 1982 to play in two of Europe's toughest leagues, Spain's Primera Division and Italy's Serie A.

Diego was at the top of his game in 1986. In the World Cup quarterfinals, Diego scored a famous game–winning goal against England. The goal was called "the Hand of God Goal" because it was a mystery how the ball ended up in the net. Well, it was a mystery to the referee. Diego actually punched the ball into the net with his hand, which is against the rules. All the world — except the ref — saw Diego's infraction. But the goal stood.

Diego also set up the winning goal in the final against Germany with a spectacular pass, and was given the Golden Ball award as the tournament's best player.

PAST STAR BOBBY CHARLTON

Bobby was a midfielder from England who had grace, speed, and a thunderbolt shot that made him dangerous even when he was 30 yards away from the goal.

In 1966, Bobby and his brother Jack became the first brothers to play for a World Cup champion. Bobby scored both goals in a 2–1 semi–final win over Portugal that sent England into the final game. England then defeated West Germany, 4–2, in overtime. Bobby was voted Best Player of the Year in England and the European Player of the Year.

Bobby finished his national team career in 1970 with what were then records for appearances (106) and goals (49) in international play. England's Queen Elizabeth honored Bobby by knighting him in 1994. He is now called Sir Bobby Charlton.

PELÉ

He has not played since 1977, but kids in Brazil still pretend to be Pelé. They dream of following in his giant footsteps, because Pelé was the greatest and most famous soccer player of all time.

Pelé was the heart and soul of the Brazilian teams that won three World Cup championships (in four tries) from 1958 to 1970. Playing the striker position, he was quick as an arrow, a wizard who could score with either foot and with his head.

Opponents' throats went dry when they thought of facing Pelé. He could turn defenders inside out with his fakes and leave the best goalies frozen in their boots as he blasted yet another wicked shot into the net. He was a master of such mind–bending moves as the bicycle kick — a backward somersault in mid–air made while kicking the ball into the net.

Pelé's real name is Edson Arantes do Nascimento. He was born on October 23, 1940, in the tiny town of Trés Coracoés, Brazil. His dad had been a pro soccer player whose career was ended by injury when Edson was a kid. Edson's family was very poor, so he had to drop out of school. He sold newspapers and shined shoes to raise money for food and clothes.

Like most kids in Brazil, Edson loved to play soccer. The boy who was called Pelé, which is simply a nickname, like "Buzz" or "Spike," used bags of rags as balls and played soccer barefoot on Brazilian beaches. He joined a junior team and led it to three regional championships.

At age 15, Pelé was invited to join a professional club team called Santos. He went on to lead the team to eight league titles, from 1958 to 1969. Pelé's stats are totally staggering. He scored 65 goals during his first season with Santos, and an unbelievable total of 126 during the 1959 season.

Pelé first played for his country as a teenager. At 17, he scored six goals in Brazil's successful 1958 World Cup campaign, including two goals in the final against Sweden. One of the goals was a Pelé specialty: With his back to the goal, Pelé knocked the ball up and over his shoulder with his thigh, quickly pivoted, and blasted the ball high into the net.

Pelé became world famous after the 1958 World Cup championship. Club teams in Europe wanted to buy him, but Brazil's government declared him an "official national treasure" and would not allow him to be traded or sold. He helped Brazil win another World Cup championship in 1970, scoring the go-ahead goal against Italy in the final game.

"The Black Pearl," as Pelé was also called, retired in 1974. Then he made a surprise comeback. He decided to come to the United States, in 1975, to join the New York Cosmos of he North American Soccer League (NASL). *(For more about the NASL, turn to page 72.)* Pelé said he came out of retirement not for money, but "to make soccer truly popular in the United States."

Pelé attracted huge crowds to the stadiums wherever the Cosmos played. He showed flashes of his old brilliance by scoring 13 goals in 22 games and winning the 1976 NASL MVP award. In 1977, Pelé led the Cosmos to the championship of the league.

He retired again after the 1977 season, having scored ,281 career goals. That is the second–highest total in history, behind Artur Friedenreich of Brazil (1,329).

Pelé holds the record for most career hat tricks (three or more goals in one game) in club team competition (92).

Pelé was a great ambassador for his sport. He often visited troubled countries. Two African nations stopped fighting a war for two days when he visited them in 1968.

Pelé called soccer the "beautiful game." We call him the game's most beautiful player.

MEN'S WORLD CUP CHAMPIONS

YEAR	WINNER	RUNNER-UP	FINAL SCORE	HOST COUNTRY
1930	Uruguay	Argentina	4-2	Uruguay
1934	Italy	Czechoslovakia	2-1 (OT)	Italy
1938	Italy	Hungary	4-2	France
1950	Uruguay	Brazil	2-1	Brazil
1954	West Germany	Hungary	3-2	Switzerland
1958	Brazil	Sweden	5-2	Sweden
1962	Brazil	Czechoslovakia	3-1	Chile
1966	England	West Germany	4-2 (OT)	England
1970	Brazil	Italy	4-1	Mexico
1974	West Germany	Netherlands	2-1	West Germany
1978	Argentina	Netherlands	3-1 (OT)	Argentina
1982	Italy	West Germany	3-1	Italy
1986	Argentina	West Germany	3-2	Mexico
1990	West Germany	Argentina	1-0	Italy
1994	Brazil	Italy	0-0 (OT)*	USA
1998	France	Brazil	3-0	France

*(Brazil won, 3–2, on penalty kicks)

ALL-TIME TEAM RANKINGS

RANK	TEAM	WON	LOST	TIED	GOALS FOR	GOALS AGAINST
1	Brazil	53	13	14	173	78
2	Germany	45	16	17	162	103
3	Italy	38	12	16	105	62
4	Argentina	29	18	10	100	69
5	England	20	12	13	62	42
31	USA	4	12	1	18	38

TOP ALL-TIME GOAL SCORERS

GOALS	PLAYER	COUNTRY
14	Gerd Muller	Germany
13	Just Fontaine	France
12	Pelé	Brazil
11	Sandor Kocsis	Hungary
11	Jurgen Klinsmann	Germany

2002 WORLD CUP TEAMS BY GROUP

GROUP A	GROUP B	GROUP C	GROUP D
France	Spain	Brazil	Portugal
Denmark	Slovenia	Turkey	United States
Uruguay	Paraguay	Costa Rica	Poland
Senegal	South Africa	China	South Korea

GROUP E	GROUP F	GROUP G	GROUP H
Germany	England	Italy	Japan
Ireland	Argentina	Ecuador	Belgium
Cameroon	Nigeria	Croatia	Russia
Saudi Arabia	Sweden	Mexico	Tunisia

CHECK IT OUT!

To get the latest news, team listings, match schedules, videos, and links to World Cup information, check out *http://www.fifaworldcup.com* on the Internet.

WOMEN'S WORLD CUP

Without a doubt, it was the biggest event in the history of women's sports. More than 650,000 tickets were sold to the 32 games that were held in seven U.S. cities during June and July 1999. More than 90,000 gonzo, screaming, flag–waving fans attended the final game. It was played in the Rose Bowl, in Pasadena, California, on July 10. Forty million TV viewers watched that game, between the United States and China. That is 29 million more than the number that watched the final game of the 1999 NBA championship series three weeks earlier.

The event was the 1999 Women's World Cup. Looking back at all the hoopla, headlines, and heroes it created, it's hard to believe that women's soccer was once thought of as little more than a novelty, not a real sport.

It's true.

FAST FACT

Women's soccer is on the rise! There are more than 30 million female soccer players of all ages in 85 countries around the world. More than seven million females play soccer in the United States. All eyes will be on the next Women's World Cup, which will be in China in 2003.

Female soccer players rarely received any attention, even though they often played the sport in England, France, and Canada during the early 1900s. In 1921, the English Football Association (F.A.) banned women from playing in its stadiums. The F.A. thought that women's soccer was more like a fun exhibition than a real game — and that the game was too tough for women, anyway.

The F.A. did not lift its ban on women until the early 1970s. Mexico City hosted an unofficial world championship for women with six amateur teams in 1971. The opening match was attended by 108,000 fans, but the game was part of a larger festival that included rodeos and baseball games. The women soccer players weren't taken seriously. They played on a field with pink goalposts!

Things began to change in 1972, when the U.S. Congress passed a law called Title IX. The law required high schools and colleges to create sports teams for girls and women.

Women's soccer began to grow in popularity. A women's world–championship tournament was held in 1988. It set the stage for a bigger and better event.

The first official Women's World Cup was held in China in 1991. The United States won. The event attracted top teams from 12 countries, but not much attention from newspapers, magazines, or TV networks. The same was true for the second Women's World Cup, which was won by Norway, in 1995.

It wasn't until the 1996 Summer Olympics that women's soccer finally began to make some major noise. (*For more on Olympic soccer, see page 35.*)

The 1996 Women's Olympic tournament attracted a lot of attention in the United States because it was held in the United States. It became an even bigger story when the United States defeated China for the gold medal. More people, especially Americans, became aware of such great players as the United States' Mia Hamm and Michelle Akers, and China's Sun [SOON] Wen.

The 1999 Women's World Cup was pure magic. Teams from 63 countries in six FIFA confederations played a grueling 141 qualifying matches to earn one of the 15 spots at the tournament, along with the host team, the United States. The final game, with its nail–biting overtime shoot–out won by the United States over China, showed just how far the women's game has come, and that it is here to stay.

LEGENDARY TEAMS

TEAM USA 1991: The U.S. women's team was led by a dominating forward line nicknamed "the Triple-edged Sword." The line included strikers Michelle Akers, Carin Jennings, and April Heinrichs. They scored a combined 20 goals as the United States crushed all six of its opponents on the way to winning the first Women's World Cup.

In the final game, Michelle capped off a super tournament by scoring both goals in a 2–1 victory over Norway. Michelle won the Golden Boot award as the tournament's top scorer. Carin won the Golden Ball as MVP. Four players from this team were on the 1999 World Cup championship team.

TEAM NORWAY 1995: This awesome defensive team was led by forward Linda Medalen. The rampaging Norwegians allowed no goals while scoring 17 in the opening round of group play. They shut out the United States in the semi-final, 1–0, and Germany, 2–0, in the final. Amazingly, Norway allowed only one goal in six games during the tournament. Midfielder Hege Riise, *(see "Star to Watch," page 32)* who scored five goals, won the Golden Ball as MVP.

STAR TO WATCH | MIA HAMM

Forward Mia Hamm keeps insisting that she's not the best player in the world. Mia was the brightest star on the U.S. team that won the 1999 Women's World Cup, but midfielder Sun Wen of China was named the tournament's Most Outstanding Player. Sun scored seven goals while Mia scored only two.

"I know I'm no better than anyone else out there," says Mia.

Whether she likes it or not, Mia is the world's most famous soccer player. She is the face and soul of women's soccer to millions of girls, the player who drives boys and girls, and even grown-ups, crazy with "Mia-mania." She has made soccer so popular in the United States that she has become a celebrity. *People* magazine named her one of the 50 Most Beautiful People in the World, in 1997. Mia even did a commercial with Michael Jordan.

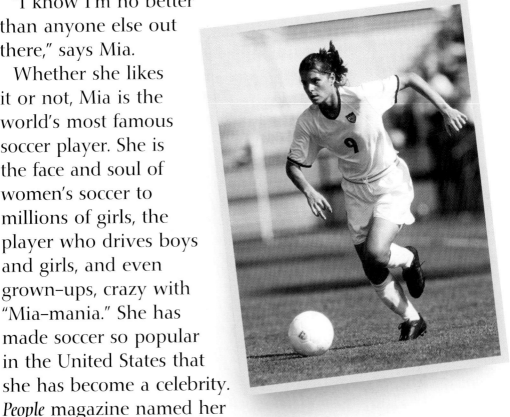

Mia's quickness, booming shot, and laser-like passing have made her the highest-scoring female player in the world. She ended 2001 as the world's all-time leading scorer with 129 goals and 109 assists. She has also won the U.S. Soccer Federation's Female Athlete of the Year award five years in a row (1994–98).

Mariel Margaret "Mia" Hamm was born on March 17, 1972, in Selma, Alabama. Her father was a colonel in the

U.S. Air Force. Mia's family often moved each time Colonel Hamm was assigned to a new Air Force base. As a kid, Mia lived in California, Texas, Virginia, and Italy.

Mia began playing soccer with her older brother, Garrett, when she was six years old. She says that she wasn't confident as a kid, but playing soccer — and being good at it — made her feel better about herself.

By age 14, Mia had become such a dominant player that she was scouted by Anson Dorrance, the head coach at the University of North Carolina (UNC). The UNC Tar Heels became a soccer powerhouse when Mia joined them. They won four National Collegiate Athletic Association (NCAA) national college championships, and Mia was a three-time All-American. She finished her college career in 1993 as UNC's all-time leader in goals (103) and points (278).

Mia was the youngest female ever to appear for the U.S. national team, which she did at the age of 15. In her outstanding national-team career, she's been on three World Cup teams, twice as a champion (1991, 1999), and is an Olympic gold and silver medal winner (1996, 2000).

Mia's reputation is now so great that she can affect a game just by stepping onto the field. Opposing defenders must concentrate so hard on stopping Mia that her teammates get more chances to score. Most of all, Mia is a true team player. Part of what makes her great is her willingness to sacrifice her own goals to help her teammates win.

Just to show you how far she'll go for her team, Mia agreed to play goalkeeper during the final minutes of a game against Denmark at the 1995 World Cup. U.S. goalie Briana Scurry had been ejected from the game, and the team had used up all of its substitutes.

Mia coolly took Briana's place and did not allow a goal.

Believe it or not, Mia doesn't volunteer to take penalty kicks because she lacks confidence. Her teammates nick-named her "Boot" because she was booted from, or kicked off, the penalty-kick squad for doing poorly in practice drills.

Reporters have said that Mia is unfriendly, but her mom says that Mia is just "shy." Mia is not the most talkative person on the U.S. team. She usually leaves the talking to her chatty teammates.

In 2000, Mia helped the U.S. team to win the silver medal at the Sydney Olympics (*see page 36*), in Australia. Her game-winning goal in the 60th minute of the semifinal match against Brazil put the United States into the gold-medal game against Norway. The Brazilian team showed Mia no mercy throughout the match. Three fouls were called on Brazilian players for knocking Mia down. Mia kept her calm and played like a true champ. Norway beat the U.S. team, 3–1, in a dramatic, tough, and well-played championship game.

Mia's efforts were recognized as she was awarded the title of FIFA World Footballer of the Year for 2001. It was the first time in soccer history that the award was given to a woman.

As always, in her quiet way, Mia accepted with modesty. "I'm just a footballer. I've not freed any slaves or changed the world. I just play football and enjoy my success," she said.

Mia is one of the founding members of the Women's United Soccer Association (WUSA), and plays for the Washington Freedom.

Mia may not believe it, but she has changed the world — the world of soccer.

STAR TO WATCH CARLA OVERBECK

Carla is the Cal Ripken, Jr. of soccer. She's a true iron woman. Her streak of playing in 63 international games in a row, from 1993 to 1996, is the U.S. national team record for women and men.

Carla played 3,547 consecutive minutes during her streak, which ended when she took time off to have a baby boy, named Jackson. Jackson stayed with Carla while the U.S. team prepared for the 1999 World Cup. That makes Carla a true soccer mom!

Carla is also a tough and steady defender who has always been a winner. She helped the University of North Carolina Tar Heels win four national college championships. She was captain of the U.S. team that won the 1996 Olympic gold medal and the 1999 World Cup.

Carla retired from the national team in 2000 after competing in the Sydney Games. She spent 13 years on the team, playing in 168 games and winning one Olympic

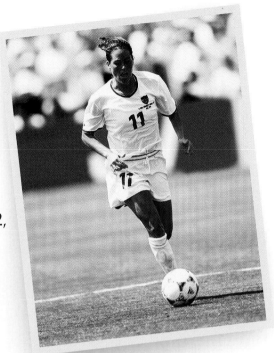

championship and two World Cup titles.

Carla is a founding member of the WUSA. In 2001, she was captain of the league's Carolina Courage, and started in every game. In early 2002, Carla underwent surgery to repair cartilage in her right knee. She hopes to return to the Courage by mid–season.

STAR TO WATCH JULIE FOUDY

Julie is the motormouthed midfielder and co–captain of the U.S. women's team. She directs the team's attack by shouting instructions to her teammates. She is bright, bubbly, and fun–loving. One of her coaches nicknamed her "Loudy Foudy" because Julie always has something to say.

Julie has played for the U.S. team since 1988, when she was 16 years old. She scored a goal and assisted on three others in six games at the 1999 World Cup tournament.

Life is full for Julie off the field. She was accepted into Stanford University's medical school. But, instead of becoming a doctor, she wants to use her gift of gab for a career in broadcasting. Julie was an analyst for ESPN during the 1998 men's World Cup.

GREATEST MOMENTS

After 120 gut-grinding, scoreless minutes, the final game of the 1999 Women's World Cup came down to a penalty-kick shoot-out. The game was finally decided after U.S. goalie Briana Scurry made a clutch save against China, and defender Brandi Chastain scored the winning penalty kick. Brandi says she went "temporarily insane" after her winning kick. Photos of her wild celebration were on the front pages of newspapers all around the world.

Playing soccer and talking about it means that Julie will keep her chatter going for years to come — just the way she wants it. "If I were quiet," Julie says, "people would think something was wrong."

Nothing was wrong with Julie at the Olympics in Sydney, Australia, in 2000. She started all five games and played every minute of each game. She scored the only United States goal in a first-round game against China. Through the end of 2001, Julie had started in 196 of the 202 national games in which she played.

Julie is a founding member of the WUSA and was captain of the San Diego Spirit in the 2001 season.

Obviously gabbing isn't Julie's only gift.

STAR TO WATCH GAO HONG

Goalkeeper Gao [GOW] Hong is the merriest member of the Chinese team. She often bursts out smiling on the field while her teammates go grimly about their business. Gao is very confident. She is as quick as a cat and has sure hands. She fearlessly throws herself into the action.

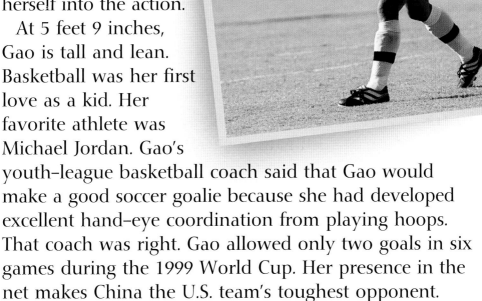

At 5 feet 9 inches, Gao is tall and lean. Basketball was her first love as a kid. Her favorite athlete was Michael Jordan. Gao's youth–league basketball coach said that Gao would make a good soccer goalie because she had developed excellent hand–eye coordination from playing hoops. That coach was right. Gao allowed only two goals in six games during the 1999 World Cup. Her presence in the net makes China the U.S. team's toughest opponent.

In 2001, Gao was drafted by the WUSA's New York Power and quickly established herself as one of the league's top goalkeepers. It was not her first time playing professionally outside of China. Gao played in a pro league for women, in Japan from 1994–97.

STAR TO WATCH   HEGE RIISE

Norwegian midfielder Hege Riise combines brains and consistency to be a dangerous offensive player. She is a seasoned veteran who acts as a model for young players to study. In fact, in Sweden, young soccer players train by watching videos of Hege in action.

Hege has more than 165 caps with the Norwegian national team. She won the gold medal in the 1995 FIFA World Cup, the Bronze medal in the 1996 Olympic games in Atlanta, Georgia, and the gold medal in the 2000 Sydney Olympics.

Hege played professionally in Japan (1995–97), and for Norway's club Sestog/Holand (1989–99) and Norway's top division side Asker (2000). She joined the WUSA's Carolina Courage in 2001, and was named the team MVP with six goals and eight assists. She is back with the Courage for the 2002 season, stronger than ever.

WOMEN'S WORLD CUP CHAMPIONS

YEAR	WINNER	RUNNER-UP	FINAL SCORE	HOST COUNTRY
1991	USA	Norway	2-1	China
1995	Norway	Germany	2-0	Sweden
1999	USA	China	0-0 (OT)*	USA

*[USA won in overtime, 5–4, on penalty kicks]

WORLD CUP INDIVIDUAL AWARDS

THE GOLDEN BALL IS AWARDED TO THE PLAYER VOTED BY THE MEDIA AS THE OUTSTANDING INDIVIDUAL COMPETITOR OF THE CHAMPIONSHIP

1991	Carin Jennings, USA
1995	Hege Riise, Norway
1999	Sun Wen, China

THE GOLDEN BOOT IS AWARDED TO THE TOP GOAL SCORER IN THE CHAMPIONSHIP

1991	Michelle Akers, USA (10 goals)
1995	Ann Kristin Aarones, Norway (six goals)
1999	Sun Wen, China (seven goals)

1999 WORLD CUP CHAMPIONSHIP ALL-STAR TEAM

DEFENDERS		MIDFIELDERS	
Wang Liping	China	Sissi	Brazil
Wen Lirong	China	Zhao Lihong	China
Doris Fitschen	Germany	Liu Ailing	China
Carla Overbeck	USA	Bettina Wiegmann	Germany
Brandi Chastain	USA	Michelle Akers	USA

GOALKEEPERS		STRIKERS	
Gao Hong	China	Jin Yan	China
Briana Scurry	USA	Sun Wen	China
		Ann Kristin Aarones	Norway
		Mia Hamm	USA

>> THE OLYMPICS

The Olympic gold medal was the ultimate prize in men's soccer until the World Cup was created in 1930. Soccer was first played as a demonstration sport at the Summer Games in 1900 and 1904. It became an official medal sport in 1908.

Until 1988, only amateur players were allowed to compete in the Olympics. The Olympic men's tournament is now considered to be the official under-23 world soccer championship. Players must be no older than 23, but three "over-age" players are allowed on each team. For example, defender Jeff Agoos was 32 when he played for the U.S. men's team in the 2000 Olympics. Men and women must be at least 16 years old to play in the Olympics.

Women's soccer became an official Olympic sport at the 1996 Summer Games, in Atlanta, Georgia. A crowd of 76,481 watched the United States defeat China for the gold medal at Sanford Stadium, in Athens, Georgia. The U.S. team's victory caused the popularity of women's soccer to skyrocket in the United States. That spark set the stage for the smashing success of the 1999 Women's World Cup and the creation of the WUSA in 2000.

SYDNEY 2000

The 2000 Summer Olympics were held in Sydney, Australia. In the men's tournament, the Americans started off strong with ties in the first round, against eventual Olympic champion Cameroon and the Czech Republic, and in the quarterfinals, against Japan. They lost to Spain in the semifinal match, 3–1, sending them to play against Chile in the battle for the bronze medal. Chile won the match, 2–0, but the United States was far from unhappy. The team had not even been expected to make it as far as they did. The fourth place finish is the U.S. men's team's best performance ever. They may not have won a medal, but they kicked off a surge of momentum that should carry them in the future.

The women's tournament in the Sydney Games was even more exciting for the U.S. team. The United States faced tough opponents Norway, China, and Nigeria before advancing to the semifinals against Brazil. The U.S. team won, 3–1, and pushed forward to the finals where they faced Norway again. Filled with emotion and intensity, this match was considered by many people as one of the best of the tournament. The United States quickly took the lead in the fifth minute of the game on

GREATEST MOMENTS

Czechoslovakia was disqualified during the 1920 gold medal game against Belgium for leaving the field to protest bad calls by the referee. Belgium was awarded the gold medal. An unusual silver medal game had to be played to determine the second-place finisher — which would have been the loser of the gold medal game if the Czechs hadn't quit. Holland and France were chosen to play. But France refused because its stars had already gone home. Spain qualified for the match by winning two more games, then it beat Holland for the silver!

a goal by Tiffeny Millbrett. Norway tied the score, 1–1, just before halftime, and then took the lead in the second half.

The game was forced into overtime when Tiffeny scored again, tying it up seconds before the end of regulation time. In the 12th minute of overtime, Dagny Mellgren of Norway scored to give her team a 3–2 gold medal victory. The U.S. team had to settle for the silver. They were disappointed in the outcome, but not in their effort.

"We're very, very proud of what we've accomplished," said defender Brandi Chastain. Added Mia Hamm, "We played our hearts out, and that in a nutshell is what our team is about. We left everything out there on the field, and you can't do anything more."

PAST STAR | MICHELLE AKERS

Midfielder Michelle Akers was the gallant warrior of the U.S. women's team. During her 15 years with the team, Michelle was carried off the field on a stretcher, and had dozens of operations on her knees. She has had so many cuts and gashes stitched up that she can't begin to remember them all. On top of all that, Michelle suffers from chronic fatigue syndrome. It's an illness that saps her energy, but it never spoiled her greatness on the field.

Michelle's teammates called her "Mufasa," the king of beasts in the movie *The Lion King.* With her lion–like mane of hair and never–say–die attitude, Michelle was the heart of the U.S. team from 1991 to 2000. She scored 10 goals in the 1991 World Cup tournament to lead her team to the title. Five of her goals were scored in one game! Michelle was given the Golden Boot award as the tournament's leading scorer.

Michelle Anne Akers was born on February 1, 1966, in Santa Clara, California. She began playing soccer when she was eight years old. Her soccer hero was the great Pelé.

Michelle's first position was goalie, but her youth–league coach switched her to center because she was an excellent ball handler. She later won All–America honors four times at the University of Central Florida. She won the 1988 College Player of the Year award.

Michelle joined the U.S. women's team in 1985, during the summer before her sophomore year in college. She scored the first goal in the team's history — against

FAST FACT

Only three teams showed up for the Olympic Soccer Tournament in 1904. Two of them were from American colleges: St. Rose and Christian Brothers. The team from St. Rose didn't have a prayer. It scored only one goal — into its own net — and finished third. A team from Canada — the Galt Football Club — won the tournament.

Denmark in 1985, and is now the team's second all-time goal scorer (104) after Mia Hamm. She was also a key member of the 1996 Olympic gold-medal-winning team.

Michelle played like a ferocious lion throughout her career. In back-to-back games in the 1999 World Cup, the tired and aching Michelle shut out the tournament's two top scorers. In the semi-final game, she stopped Brazil's sizzling scoring sensation, Sissi, in her tracks, and netted a key penalty kick in the United States' 2–0 win. In the final game, Michelle prevented China's high-powered star Sun Wen from scoring. The United States won that game, too.

Michelle gave so much of herself in the final game that a collision with teammate Briana Scurry put her out of the game at the end of regulation time in the second half. Michelle's teammates hung in there without her,

GREATEST MOMENTS

Forward Nwankwo Kanu of Nigeria's men's team scored a "golden" goal to beat Brazil, 4–3, in overtime at the 1996 Olympic semi-final game.

Brazil had been expected to win the gold medal, but Nigeria's Super Eagles made the Brazilians look like turkeys. Kanu's goal in the last minute of regulation time sent the game into OT. When Kanu scored the game-winner, he celebrated by doing a funky-chicken dance, and his teammates joined in. They were quite a sight! Never before had the world seen a team of Super Eagles turn into funky chickens.

The Nigerian media called the Super Eagles "the Dream Team" for reaching the gold-medal game. Sure enough, the Super Eagles made the dream come true by beating Argentina, 3–2, to win the gold. The game was played at Athens, Georgia, in front of 86,117 excited fans. Nigeria became the first African team to win an Olympic gold medal. Kanu is now a star for Arsenal, in England's Premier league.

defeating China in a dramatic, overtime penalty–kick shoot–out. Michelle was totally exhausted, but she returned from the locker room to join her teammates in their joyful victory celebration.

In 1998, Michelle was awarded FIFA's highest honor, the Order of Merit, for her contributions to the game.

Only three weeks before she was to compete in the 2000 Olympics, Michelle retired from the United States national team. After years of struggling with chronic fatigue syndrome and an ongoing shoulder injury, Michelle was physically and mentally exhausted. She is one of the greatest players in the history of women's soccer and her presence on the field is truly missed.

STAR TO WATCH BRIANA SCURRY

In 1996, Briana promised her teammates that she would run naked in the streets of Athens, Georgia, if the U.S. team won the Olympic gold medal. They did and Briana had to live up to her promise. She ran about 20 yards in the middle of the night when no one was around, but she kept her promise. When Briana makes up her mind, there's no stopping her!

Briana became famous when she made a gutsy save on a penalty kick against China in the 1999 World Cup final game. Her save was the difference in the game as the United States won the overtime penalty–kick shoot–out, 5–4.

The U.S. team made Briana its first–string goalie in 1994. She has more victories (79) and shutouts (54) than any other national team goalie in history. She is also the first female goalie ever to win Olympic and World Cup championships. No wonder she's considered to be the best goalkeeper in the world.

Briana's teammates play with great confidence when she is guarding their net. "We defenders are going to make mistakes, but knowing that Bri's behind us makes all the difference in the world," says Carla Overbeck, formerly the team's captain.

At 5–foot–8, Bri is not tall for a goalie. She makes up for her lack of height by being quick, cool under pressure, and fearless. She throws herself at the ball or into crowds of players. Diving into crowds was something Briana did a lot while growing up in Dayton, Minnesota. She was the youngest of nine kids, and she played a lot of sports with her siblings and friends, including tackle football. "I liked the whole idea of being tough and aggressive," she says.

When Briana took up soccer in fourth grade, she played goalie during her first year — on an all–boys team. Later, as the star goalie of the University of Massachusetts' women's team, she had 37 shutouts in 65 starts and a tiny 0.56 goals–against–per–game average. She graduated in 1995 with a degree in political science. She's athletic *and* smart.

Off the field, Bri is quiet. On the field, she's all business. Her teammates say she has a death stare when she looks into the eyes of her opponents. It's a look that says "This is my goal area. Don't mess with me!"

Of course, if her stare fails, Briana can always scare them by showing them the black panther tattoo she has on her shoulder.

Briana faced injuries in the season leading up to the 2000 Olympic Games. She ended up losing her starting spot on the national team to Siri Mullinix and played in only three matches total that year.

In 2001, Bri was a shining star as a founding member of the WUSA. She recorded the best goal's against average (.82) and best winning percentage (66.7), for a goalie, playing for the Atlanta Beat.

STAR TO WATCH SISSI

Brazil's star midfielder, Sissi, has amazing moves in her bag of tricks. Her super jukes, fakes, and swerves throw defenders into chaos. Sissi is also the best free–kicker in women's soccer. She blasts powerful shots that often curve sharply and fool goalkeepers. It is fitting that Sissi wears the famous number–10 jersey that all great Brazilian players, including Pelé, have worn.

Sissi was a key member of Brazil's 1995 and 1998 South American championship teams. At the 1996 Olympics, she scored a goal against Germany that earned Brazil a

1–1 tie and a place in the semi-final game against China. Brazil almost beat China, losing a 2–1 lead in the final seven minutes, and the game, 3–2.

Sissi sparkled at the 1999 World Cup. She scored seven goals to share the tournament scoring lead with China's Sun Wen. As for Brazil's surprising third–place finish in the World Cup, Sissi says, "We will aim higher next time."

Next time was the 2000 Olympics. After helping Brazil take fourth place in the Olympics in 2000, Sissi came to the United States to play in the WUSA. She starred for the CyberRays, starting in 20 games during the 2001 season.

STAR TO WATCH SUN WEN

Forward Sun Wen is China's team captain. She wears number 9, just like Mia Hamm. Sun set the 1999 World Cup on fire with her electric dashes and scoring skill. Her seven goals shared the scoring lead with Brazil's Sissi, but Sun was voted the tournament's Most Outstanding Player.

Sun often starts her runs from midfield, where she can pick up steam as she gets lost in a crowd. That makes it difficult for opponents to keep track of her. Sun is very fast and decisive. She has a wickedly accurate shot and tremendous playmaking skills. What's more, she's a superb free–kicker.

Sun led China to second–place finishes at the 1996 Olympics and the 1999 World Cup tournament.

She scored two goals and directed the attack when China thrashed defending World Cup champion Norway, 5–0, in the 1999 Cup semi-final. China later lost the final game to the United States in an overtime shoot-out.

Sun looked forward to a rematch with her greatest rival, Mia Hamm, at the Sydney Games. China and the United States faced each other in the preliminary round of the competition. The United States scored in the 38th minute of the game, taking the lead. Sun tied it with a spectacular free kick in the 67th minute after a foul by Mia. The match ended in a tie, but China was later knocked out of the running for a medal by Norway.

Sun joined the WUSA's Atlanta Beat for the league's first season in 2001, but played in only 13 games due to injuries.

LEGENDARY TEAM

HUNGARY

Olympic soccer was once dominated by the "Magnificent Magyars." They were a team from Hungary that won the Olympic gold medal three times between 1952 and 1968. (Magyars are the people who make up most of Hungary's population.)

The star of Hungary's first gold-medal-winning team was its captain: a short, stubby, potbellied striker named Ferenc Puskas. Ferenc didn't look like a great soccer player, but he had an amazing ability to analyze the action on the field. He directed his team's attack like an army general. Actually, Ferenc was a major in the Hungarian army. Soccer fans called him "the galloping major."

Led by Ferenc, the Magnificent Magyars were undefeated in international play from 1950 to 1954. They took on a team of England's best players in a match on May 23, 1954. The game was played in Budapest, Hungary. The Magnificent Magyars thrilled 92,000 of their countrymen by crushing England, 7–1.

Hungary failed to qualify for the 1956 Olympics. But they came back in style, winning the bronze medal in 1960 and the gold in 1964 and 1968. Hungary almost made it three golds in a row in 1972, but they were blown away in the final game.

Really, blown away.

The game was played in Munich, Germany, in a driving, raging windstorm and rainstorm. Hungary had lost only once in its last 21 Olympic matches. Its opponent that day was Poland. Hungary led, 1–0, after the first half. Then the teams switched ends of the field. The Polish team had the howling wind at its back for the entire second half. That wind helped two Polish shots find the back of the net, and Hungary was defeated, 2–1.

Hungary has yet to win another gold medal, but it has still won more Olympic soccer gold medals (three) than any other nation.

STAR TO WATCH KRISTINE LILLY

Midfielder Kristine Lilly of the United States is soccer's most "capped" player. That means that she has played for her country's national team in more international games than any other player, male or female. (The expression capped comes from England, where players used to receive real caps each time they played for England's national team.) Kristine achieved her 200th "cap" with the U.S. women's team on May 7, 2000, in Portland, Oregon.

Kristine is a tireless runner who is always on the move. She has set up many of Mia Hamm's goals. Kristine and Mia were teammates on the University of North Carolina Tar Heels team that won four NCAA championships.

Kristine has played on the U.S. teams that have won an Olympic gold medal (1996), an Olympic silver medal (2000), and World Cup championships in 1991 and 1999.

In 2000, Kristine scored six goals with five assists, including one at the Olympics in Sydney, in a match against Nigeria. Through 2001, she totaled 65 career assists and started an amazing 218 of the 228 games in which she played for the national team.

Kristine is a founding member of the WUSA and captain of the Boston Breakers.

WOMEN'S OLYMPIC CHAMPIONS

YEAR	GOLD	SILVER	BRONZE
1996	United States	China	Norway
2000	Norway	United States	Germany

MEN'S OLYMPIC CHAMPIONS

YEAR	GOLD	SILVER	BRONZE
1900	England	France	Belgium
1904	Canada	USA	USA
1906	Denmark	Int (International team)	Greece
1908	England	Denmark	Holland
1912	England	Denmark	Holland
1916	Tournament not held		
1920	Belgium	Spain	Holland
1924	Uruguay	Switzerland	Sweden
1928	Uruguay	Argentina	Italy
1932	Tournament not held		
1936	Italy	Austria	Norway

YEAR	GOLD	SILVER	BRONZE
1940	Tournament not held		
1944	Tournament not held		
1948	Sweden	Yugoslavia	Denmark
1952	Hungary	Yugoslavia	Sweden
1956	Soviet Union	Yugoslavia	Bulgaria
1960	Yugoslavia	Denmark	Hungary
1964	Hungary	Czechoslovakia	East Germany
1968	Hungary	Bulgaria	Japan
1972	Poland	Hungary	East Germany
1976	East Germany	Poland	Soviet Union
1980	Czechoslovakia	East Germany	Soviet Union
1984	France	Brazil	Yugoslavia
1988	Soviet Union	Brazil	Germany
1992	Spain	Poland	Ghana
1996	Nigeria	Argentina	Brazil
2000	Cameroon	Spain	Chile

>> THE U.S. GAME

It took Americans about 170 years to really like soccer. The sport was introduced to America by European settlers. It has been played in the United States since 1827.

Soccer was popular enough by 1884 that the American Football Association was formed to govern amateur and school teams in the United States. In 1885, teams from the United States and Canada played the first international soccer matches held outside England. The first pro league in the United States was formed in 1933. But pro soccer and major events such as the World Cup were usually greeted with yawns by most American sports fans until the mid–1990s.

When the men's World Cup tournament was held in the United States for the first time, in 1994, Americans had another chance to see how exciting top–level soccer can be. The success of that World Cup led to the creation of the pro league, Major League Soccer (MLS).

The excitement grew when the United States won the 1999 Women's World Cup, also held in the United States. American kids now wear jerseys with the names of such U.S. stars as Mia Hamm and Cobi Jones on the back. The women's national victory in 1999 helped pave the way for the birth of the WUSA in February, 2000 (*see page 69*).

About 18 million people in the United States play soccer in youth leagues, high schools, and colleges. More kids play soccer in the United States than in any other country. Soccer is popular in the United States at last. It just took us a while to learn what the rest of the world already knew: Soccer rocks.

MAJOR LEAGUE SOCCER

Major League Soccer was born in 1996 to bring top-level soccer to the United States every year. MLS develops young American players for the U.S. national team, and gives America's best young players a place to play in their home country against professional competition. Before MLS, America's best college players usually had to go to England, other countries in Europe, or South America to continue their careers. The MLS helped bring back American stars such as Landon Donovan, Eric Wynalda, and Cobi Jones, who had been playing overseas. Young Americans such as Ben Olsen, Zach Thornton, and Eddie Pope stayed in the United States and became stars by playing for MLS teams.

The MLS has 10 teams. Each team plays 28 games during the regular season (March through September). There is a mid-season All-Star Game, playoffs, and a championship game in October.

At least two pro soccer leagues in America have failed in the past because not enough fans were interested. But MLS looks as if it is here to stay. Attendance for the 2001 season totaled about 2.5 million fans, with an average of 14,964 fans per game.

STAR TO WATCH MARCO ETCHEVERRY

His nickname is "El Diablo." That's Spanish for "the Devil." Marco Etcheverry was given the nickname because of the intense look he gets in his eyes during a game. But to his fans and teammates, Marco is more like a soccer god than a devil.

El Diablo burns his opponents with his wicked dribbling and fiery passion for the game. He jukes and spins and sets up teammates for goals with crisp, accurate passes. He has a deadly shot that curves like a banana. He's strong. Opponents have a devil of a time taking the ball away from him.

FAST FACT

Their Cups Runneth Over!

MLS teams often play in Cup competitions against pro teams from foreign countries. The MLS champion competes each year in the CONCACAF Cup. This is a tournament for teams from North and Central America and the Caribbean. D.C. United was the first MLS team to win the Cup, beating Toluca of Mexico in 1998. D.C. also beat South American club champs Vasco da Gama in the 1998 InterAmerica Cup. The Chicago Fire won the annual U.S. Open Cup in 1998 and 2000. The Los Angeles Galaxy won in 2001. It is the oldest Cup competition in U.S. soccer. It was first played in 1914 and is open to all amateur and pro teams in the United States.

Marco is one of the best players in MLS. As the star midfielder for D.C. United, he is the foundation of the team's championship dynasty. Marco's masterful playmaking has sparked D.C. United to three MLS championships in the league's first four seasons. He is the all–time MLS leader in assists with 86, a four–time All–Star, and the 1998 MLS MVP.

Marco was born on September 26, 1970, in Santa Cruz, Bolivia. He graduated from Bolivia's world–famous Tahuichi Soccer Academy and later became captain of Bolivia's national team. Marco competed in major international competitions, but it wasn't until he joined MLS, in 1996, that the world really noticed his outstanding talent.

A pinpoint corner kick by Marco set up the game-winning, overtime goal in the 1996 MLS championship game against the Los Angeles Galaxy. Marco's kick was headed into the net by his teammate, defender Eddie Pope. D.C. United won, 3–2. Marco was selected as the Most Valuable Player of the game.

Marco was a finalist for the MLS MVP award in 1997, even though he missed almost half the season while playing for Bolivia's national team in World Cup qualifying matches. In 1998, he scored 10 goals and set the MLS single-season record of 19 assists. He was such a dominant playmaker that he recorded points in 22 of the 29 regular-season games he played. In 1999, he scored a goal and set up three more while leading D.C. United past the Columbus Crew, 4–0, in the 1999 Eastern Conference playoff final. Then he led D.C. to its third MLS Cup victory, over the Galaxy.

In 2001, El Diablo led D.C. in minutes played with 2,024 and led the MLS in corner kicks with 115 in 23 games. He is the league's all-time assist leader with 86, and earned Player of the Week honors for the week ending March 31, 2002. In early 2002, Marco signed a contract with MLS that should keep him in Washington for the rest of his career.

Marco is fearless on a soccer field. "I don't worry much about my opponents," he says. "Let *them* worry about me."

That they do. The fear of the devil is in everyone who plays against El Diablo.

STAR TO WATCH MAURICIO CIENFUEGOS

Midfielder Mauricio Cienfuegos is one of the Los Angeles Galaxy's brightest stars. He is the spark that jump-starts the team's dynamic offense. The Galaxy set an MLS single-season record of 85 goals in 1998.

Mauricio often sets up goals for scorers such as midfielder Cobi Jones. He has led the Galaxy in assists every year. Mauricio's 23 points in 1999 made him the

FAST FACT

The Chicago Fire made history by blazing its way to a surprising double championship in 1998. As a first-year team, the Fire wasn't expected to be so hot. Chicago stunned the soccer world by reaching, and winning, the MLS championship game with a 2–0 victory over two-time defending champs, D.C. United. The win made the Fire the only expansion team in any sport ever to win a major championship in its first season. The Fire completed its double by defeating the Columbus Crew, 2–1, in the 1998 U.S. Open Cup final.

team's second-leading point scorer, after Cobi. In 1999, his career total of 21 game-winning assists was the league's best, and through 2001, he had reached 24.

Mauricio was born in the Central American country of El Salvador. He was the captain of its national team until he retired in 1998. He currently plays for the Galaxy and has played in all five MLS All-Star Games.

STAR TO WATCH ROY LASSITER

Flashy striker Roy Lassiter is known for imitating an airplane whenever he scores a goal. Roy had plenty of chances to practice his "flying" during his first six seasons in MLS. As the league's all-time leading scorer, he has 88 goals in 165 games for the Tampa Bay Mutiny, D.C. United, and the Kansas City Wizards. He is second in game-winning goals (19), and third in shots on goal (324).

Roy uses his tremendous speed to get behind defenses. He's a deadly finisher who loves smashing the ball past despairing goaltenders. Roy won the 1996 MLS Golden Boot award as the league's leading goal scorer, with 27 goals in 30 regular-season games. He scored six more in five post-season games. In 1999, he tied for the goal-scoring lead with 18 goals for D.C. United.

Roy joined with the Miami Fusion for the 2000 season, finishing second on the team in goals (eight) and points (25). He was traded to the Kansas City Wizards for the 2001 season, where he scored his 200th career MLS point.

STAR TO WATCH JASON KREIS

One of the hottest stars on the Dallas Burn is Jason Kreis. A fifth-round draft pick in 1996, the high-scoring midfielder was the Burn's all-time leader in goals (66) and assists (57) at the start of the 2002 season.

In 1999, Jason was named the MLS MVP and won the league's scoring title with 18 goals and 15 assists for 51 points. The next season, he led the Burn in scoring with 11 goals and 13 assists for 35 points. He became the fourth player in league history to register 50 career goals. Jason's 189 points in 2001 made him the fourth all-time leading scorer in MLS history. He is third all-time in goals, with 66.

Jason obviously has a knack for popping up in the right place at the right time and booming a shot pass the startled goalie. Many of Jason's goals have sent the Burn into their locker room to celebrate a victory. At the beginning of the 2002 season, he was leading the league in game-winning goals (22).

STAR TO WATCH COBI JONES

Cobi is one of America's most famous soccer stars. He became well-known for his dreadlocked hair and nifty goal-scoring as a midfielder for the U.S. men's team in the 1994 World Cup tournament. Cobi is one of only two members of the U.S. team who played in every game of the 1994 and 1998 World Cups.

Cobi is also the youngest man in the world to appear in 100 international games. He reached that milestone at age 27 in the U.S. team's 1–0 upset win over world champion Brazil in a 1998 game. By the end of 2001, Cobi ranked fifth on the all–time international cap–winners list with 145.

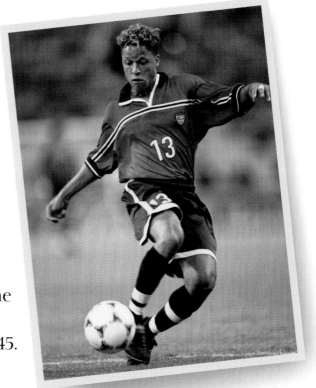

MLS fans know Cobi as a key member of the Los Angeles Galaxy's high–powered offense. He was named the U.S. Soccer Athlete of the Year after he scored 19 goals and had 13 assists for the Galaxy in 1998. He was the team's top scorer in 1998 and 1999. As the team captain, Cobi led the Galaxy in scoring for the fourth consecutive year in 2001.

When he is not blasting goals for the Galaxy or the national team, Cobi has often appeared on MTV and in TV shows such as *Beverly Hills 90210*.

STAR TO WATCH BEN OLSEN

Ben is one of the many talented young Americans who are getting their professional start in MLS. He is an attack–minded midfielder who challenges opponents with his speed and dribbling skill.

Before joining MLS in 1998 at age 21, Ben scored 34 goals and passed for 41 assists at the University of Virginia.

He was named the 1997 Soccer America College Player of the Year. In his first MLS season, Ben won the 1998 Rookie of the Year award. He scored the clinching goal for D.C. United in the 1999 MLS Cup final, and was the game's MVP.

In 2000, Ben pulled triple duty with D.C. United, the U.S. Men's National Team, and the U.S. Under–23 men's team. He played in the 2000 Summer Olympics, helping the U.S. team to a fourth–place finish. Unfortunately, Ben missed the entire 2001 MLS season after fracturing his ankle in March of that year.

STAR TO WATCH ZACH THORNTON

Zach is nicknamed "the Beast" because he is big (6 feet 3 inches, 210 pounds) and he has a large appetite. He loves stuffing himself with barbecued steaks or his mom's crab cakes.

The Beast is one of the top goalkeepers in MLS. He had a huge year in 1998. Zach had rarely played in two seasons as the backup for the New York/New Jersey MetroStars. Then he was chosen by the Chicago Fire in the 1998 MLS expansion draft. (The Fire was a new team.) Zach won the starting job, made the All-Star team, and had the lowest goals-against average (1.17) in MLS history. He led the league with eight regular-season shutouts and posted three more buckets of whitewash in the playoffs. And he was named the 1998 MLS Goalkeeper of the Year. Wait, there's more!

Zach backstopped the Fire to victory over D.C. United in the MLS championship. To top off his year, he made his first appearance for the U.S. national team, against Australia.

In 2000, Zach helped Chicago advance to the MLS Cup against Kansas City, who won 1-0. Zach was named Chicago's Defender of the Year in 2001, and was the only Fire player to play every minute of every game that year. With Zach's kind of dedication, the Fire will surely remain hot.

STAR TO WATCH EDDIE POPE

Using his head to make good things happen is Eddie's specialty. His greatest moment as a professional came when he headed the ball into the net for a game-winning goal in the 1996 MLS championship game. Eddie's heady score gave D.C. United the first of its three MLS Cups. He played on all three of those championship teams.

Eddie is a smart defender. He is often assigned to shut down the opposing team's best scorer. He was named the 1997 MLS Defender of the Year and won the 1997 Player of the Year award as the top player in the United States.

Eddie is also a member of the U.S. Men's National Team. He appeared in every game the United States played in the 1996 Olympics and 1998 World Cup. He scored the winning goal for D.C. United in the 1998 InterAmerican Cup. The victory earned his team the title of "Champion of the Americas." It also attracted interest in Eddie from Dutch and Italian teams, who would love to have him use his head in their leagues.

Eddie's 1999 and 2000 seasons with D.C. United were disappointing due to injuries. He underwent surgery on his knee before the start of the 2001 season, but came back strong and was named the club's top defender of the year for the third time in his six-year career.

STAR TO WATCH JOHN HARKES

John has been a part of nearly every major event in the history of U.S. soccer. As captain and midfielder, John helped the U.S. Men's National Team qualify for the 1990 and 1998 World Cup tournaments. He also helped the team compete as the host of the 1994 World Cup.

John is one of the most successful Americans ever to have played overseas. "Harksey," as he was called by fans

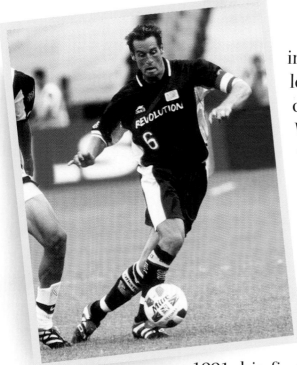

in England, played top-level soccer for an English club team, called Sheffield Wednesday, from 1991 until 1996.

When John first arrived in England, fans yelled "Yankee, go home!" But John won the fans' hearts when he helped Sheffield Wednesday win the English League Cup in 1991, his first season with the team.

John returned to America in 1996 to help kick–start MLS. He was captain of D.C. United when it won the first two MLS Cup championships (1996 and 1997). He also led D.C. to victory in the 1998 InterAmerican Cup championship.

John spent 1999 and 2000 with the New England Revolution. As captain in 2000, he led the team to its best season ever, with an all–time season–high point total of 45. He was traded in mid–season of 2001 to the Columbus Crew.

PAST STAR ERIC WYNALDA

Eric earned the distinction of scoring the first goal in MLS history. He did it on April 6, 1996, for the San Jose Clash against D.C. United.

Eric was a striker who could score with both feet and his head. Those skills helped him excel in international competition. Eric was the first American–born player to play in Germany's famous Bundesliga. (*For more on the Bundesliga, see page 88.*) Eric scored nine goals in his first 10 matches with the team FC Saarbruecken, in 1992.

Like John Harkes, Eric returned to America from overseas to kick off MLS in 1996. He scored 10 goals and had 13 assists for the Clash that season, and he was named the 1996 U.S. Soccer Player of the Year.

Eric was also a key member of the U.S. Men's National Team. He was the team's all–time goal scorer, with 33 goals in 102 games. That is almost one goal in every three games! Eric has also appeared in three World Cups (1990, 1994, and 1998).

Eric played for the Miami Fusion from 1999 through mid–2000 when he was traded to the New England Revolution. He began 2001 with the Chicago Fire, but was traded back to the Revolution for the end of the season.

STAR TO WATCH CARLOS VALDERRAMA

With his big, wild mane of flaming orange hair, Carlos would stand out on any soccer field. Soccer fans love his colorful 'do.

"My hair is a symbol of my personality," he says.

MLS wanted colorful, talented players when it started play in 1996. With his fancy footwork and wild hair,

Carlos was perfect. His dazzling skills have made him one of the league's best-known stars. Nicknamed El Pibe ("the Kid"), Carlos is famous for his joy, creativity, and pinpoint passing. He is a master of the "one-touch" pass. He receives the ball and instantly sends it to a teammate. At the start of the 2002 season, Carlos ranked first all-time in assists (98).

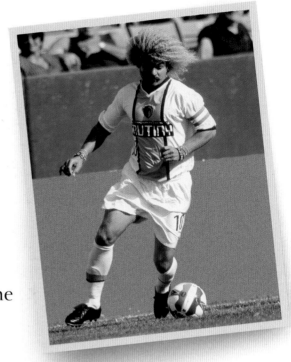

Carlos grew up in a poor area of Santa Marta, Colombia. He learned to play soccer using a ball made of rags. His dad had been a pro soccer player. Carlos began his career in Colombia in 1981. He played club soccer in South America, France, and Spain before he brought his great talent and experience to the Tampa Bay Mutiny in 1996. He immediately set MLS on fire with his playmaking. Carlos co-led the league in assists with 19, and he was named the 1996 MLS MVP. He was the MLS All-Star Game MVP in 1996 and 1997.

Carlos spent 1998 and 1999 with the Miami Fusion before he was traded back to Tampa Bay. He was traded to the Colorado Rapids in 2001. He is the first active player over 40 years old in MLS history.

MLS CHAMPIONS

MLS CUP '01 (OT)

San Jose Earthquakes 2, Los Angeles Galaxy 1

MVP Dwayne DeRosario, San Jose Earthquakes

MLS CUP '00

Kansas City Wizards 1, Chicago Fire 0

MVP Tony Meola, Kansas City Wizards

MLS CUP '99

D.C. United 2, Los Angeles Galaxy 0

MVP Ben Olsen, D.C. United

MLS CUP '98

Chicago Fire 2, D.C. United 0

MVP Peter Nowak, Chicago Fire

MLS CUP '97

D.C. United 2, Colorado Rapids 1

MVP Jamie Moreno, D.C. United

MLS CUP '96

D.C. United 3, Los Angeles Galaxy 2 (OT)

MVP Marco Etcheverry, D.C. United

ALL-TIME LEADERS

SCORERS

RANK	NAME	TEAM	GAMES	GOALS	ASSISTS	POINTS
1	Roy Lassiter	KC	165	88	35	211
2	Preki	TB	169	58	83	199
3	Raul Diaz Arce	COL	150	82	29	193
4	Jason Kreis	DAL	177	66	57	189
5	Jaime Moreno	DC	134	66	48	180
6	Cobi Jones	LA	153	54	50	158
7	Ronald Cerritos	SJ	118	55	38	148
8	Diego Serna	MET	100	52	36	140
9	Marco Etcheverry	DC	142	25	86	136
10	Mauricio Cienfuegos	LA	163	33	70	136

GOALKEEPING LEADERS (Minimum 4500 minutes)

RANK	NAME	TEAMS	GP	GAA	RECORD	SO
1	Kevin Hartman	LA	106	1.12	62-33-8	32
2	Zach Thornton	CHI	113	1.23	66-33-11	29
3	Joe Cannon	SJ	75	1.31	33-29-13	18
4	Tony Meola	KC	147	1.46	63-73-11	41
5	Mark Simpson	DC	53	1.49	26-18-4	9
6	Matt Jordan	DAL	87	1.51	40-37-9	27
7	Mark Dodd	DAL	92	1.57	44-45-0	16
8	Marcus Hahnemann	COL	66	1.59	39-25-0	13
9	Scott Garlick	COL	125	1.60	64-50-9	21
10	Tom Presthus	CLB	147	1.46	63-73-11	41

AWARD WINNERS

MOST VALUABLE PLAYER

SEASON	PLAYER	TEAM
2001	Alex Pineda Chacon*	Miami Fusion
2000	Tony Meola	Kansas City Wizards
1999	Jason Kreis	Dallas Burn
1998	Marco Etcheverry	D.C. United
1997	Preki	Kansas City Wizards
1996	Carlos Valderrama**	Tampa Bay Mutiny

  * now with New England Revolution

** now with Colarado Rapids

GOALKEEPER OF THE YEAR

SEASON	PLAYER	TEAM
2001	Tim Howard	NY/NJ MetroStars
2000	Tony Meola	Kansas City Wizards
1999	Kevin Hartman	Los Angeles Galaxy
1998	Zach Thornton	Chicago Fire
1997	Brad Friedel	Columbus Crew
1996	Mark Dodd	Dallas Burn

AWARD WINNERS

ROOKIE OF THE YEAR

SEASON	PLAYER	TEAM
2001	Rodrigo Faria	NY/NJ MetroStars
2000	Carlos Bocanegra	Chicago Fire
1999	Jay Heaps	Miami Fusion
1998	Ben Olsen	D.C. United
1997	Mike Duhaney	Tampa Bay Mutiny
1996	Steve Ralston	Tampa Bay Mutiny

DEFENDER OF THE YEAR

SEASON	PLAYER	TEAM
2001	Jeff Agoos	San Jose Earthquakes
2000	Peter Vermes	Kansas City Wizards
1999	Robin Fraser	Los Angeles Galaxy
1998	Lubos Kubik	Chicago Fire
1997	Eddie Pope	D.C. United
1996	John Doyle	San Jose Clash

NEWSFLASH!

In January of 2002, the Commissioner of Major League Soccer, Don Garber, announced that the Miami Fusion and the Tampa Bay Mutiny would be eliminated from the league. The players were assigned to other teams in drafts that month. According to Mr. Garber, the change was, "necessary to ensure the future success of the League."

WOMEN'S UNITED SOCCER ASSOCIATION

Professional women's soccer made its debut in the United States in 2001 with the birth of the WUSA. After the excitement of the 1996 Olympic and 1999 World Cup tournaments, interest in women's soccer had risen to a new level. Female soccer players demonstrated supreme skills and a passion for the game that demanded the world's attention. Women's soccer was no longer a novelty act. It was time for it to be taken seriously.

In February 2000, plans were announced to begin play in 2001. The 20 members of the 1999 Women's World Cup Championship team became the founding players

THE GREAT EIGHT

The teams that make up the WUSA are:

ATLANTA BEAT

SAN JOSE CYBERRAYS*

BOSTON BREAKERS

CAROLINA COURAGE

NEW YORK POWER

PHILADELPHIA CHARGE

SAN DIEGO SPIRIT

WASHINGTON FREEDOM

*changed name from Bay Area CyberRays on November 7, 2001

of the WUSA (*see box on page 72*). They were joined by national newcomers and major stars from around the world to play in the eight-team league (*see box above*). The 21-game first season was kicked off in April and ran through August 2001. An opening ceremony was held, highlighted by an appearance by women's sport's activist and tennis legend, Billie Jean King. The season was a successful debut, with an average of over 8,000 fans attending each game.

2001 WUSA FINAL STANDINGS

TEAM	W	L	T	POINTS
Atlanta	10	4	7	37
Bay Area	11	6	4	37
Philadelphia	9	8	4	31
New York	9	7	5	32
San Diego	7	7	7	28
Boston	8	10	3	27
Washington	6	12	2	21
Carolina	6	12	2	21

LEAGUE CHAMPIONS Bay Area CyberRays

2001 TOP SCORERS

POINTS LEADERS

NAME	TEAM	POINTS
Tiffeny Millbrett	New York	35
Shannon MacMillan	San Diego	30
Charmaine Hooper	Atlanta	27

GOALS AGAINST LEADERS

NAME	TEAM	GOALS AGAINST AVERAGE
Briana Scurry	Atlanta	.82
LaKeysia Beene	Bay Area	.97
Melissa Moore	Philadelphia	1.01

WUSA FOUNDING MEMBERS

The 20 WUSA Founding Players are the 20 members of the 1999 U.S. Women's World Cup Championship Team. They are:

Michelle Akers
Brandi Chastain
Tracy Ducar
Lorrie Fair

Joy Fawcett
Danielle Fotopoulos
Julie Foudy
Mia Hamm
Kristine Lilly
Shannon MacMillan
Tiffeny Milbrett
Carla Overbeck
Cindy Parlow
Christie Pearce
Tiffany Roberts
Briana Scurry
Kate Sobrero
Tisha Venturini-Hoch
Saskia Webber
Sara Whalen

In the hopes of inspiring a new generation of soccer stars, WUSA Founding Member Danielle Fotopoulos greets her fans before a game. Danielle is a forward for the Carolina Courage.

PAST LEAGUES: NASL AND MISL

Major League Soccer isn't America's first pro soccer league. That distinction belongs to the American Soccer League, which was founded in 1933. The most famous was the North American Soccer League (NASL).

LEGENDARY TEAM

The New York Cosmos were the Dream Team of soccer. Their lineup included such all-time greats as Pelé and Carlos Alberto of Brazil, Franz Beckenbauer of Germany, and Giorgio Chinaglia of Italy.

Pelé and defender Carlos Alberto had starred on Brazil's 1970 World Cup championship team. Franz had been captain of West Germany's World Cup championship team in 1974. For the Cosmos, Franz played defense and midfield and directed the team's attack. Striker Giorgio Chinaglia had starred with the Italian club Lazio before joining the Cosmos in 1976. Giorgio scored seven goals for the Cosmos in one game in 1980.

The Cosmos won four NASL championships in six years, from 1977 to 1982. Soccer may never see a team like that again.

The NASL was created after the 1966 World Cup. The heart-stopping final game between England and West Germany was shown on TV in the United States. Many Americans were excited by what they saw, and a pro league was formed to take advantage of the new interest in soccer. The NASL began with six teams: two from Canada (Vancouver and Toronto) and four from the United States (Detroit, New York, Tampa, and San Diego). The league grew to 20 teams by 1975.

The NASL played its first season in 1968. Stars from around the world came to the league. It attracted world-wide interest when the legendary Pelé came out of retirement to play for the New York Cosmos, in 1975.

Crowds of more than 70,000 people regularly filled Giants Stadium, in the New Jersey Meadowlands, to watch the Cosmos and their all-star lineup (*see box on page 73*). But the excitement lasted only two years. After Pelé retired, in 1977, fans began to lose interest. Attendance shrank. The league had to compete for fans and players with the faster-paced indoor soccer leagues. The NASL went out of business in 1984.

INDOOR LEAGUES

Indoor soccer is like pinball. It's full of fast-paced action and crazy bounces. The game is played on artificial turf. The field (about 200 feet long and 85 feet wide) is smaller than a regular soccer field (100 to 130 yards long and 50 to 100 yards wide). The indoor field is surrounded by boards topped by Plexiglas, which make the field look like a hockey rink. Players bank shots and passes off the walls.

Each indoor goal is set into the boards at either end of the field. (Outdoor goals are nets hung from goalposts.) An indoor game has four 15-minute quarters instead of 45-minute halves. Each team has a goalkeeper, but an indoor team has only five field players. An outdoor team has 10.

America's first indoor league was the Major Indoor Soccer League (MISL). It kicked off in 1978. Some teams attracted as many as 10,000 fans per game. The MISL got caught in costly bidding wars for top players with the outdoor NASL and the rival American Indoor Soccer Association, which later became the National Professional Soccer League (NPSL). The high price of the best players drove the MISL out of business in 1991. A few of its teams joined the NPSL, which then changed its name to MISL in 2001. The MISL began the season with six teams: Baltimore Blast, Cleveland Crunch, Harrisburg Heat, Kansas City Comets, and Philadelphia Kixx.

In December 2001, MISL merged with the World Indoor Soccer League (WISL). Three teams would be joining MISL: Dallas SideKicks, San Diego Soccers, and St. Louis Steamers.

Outdoor-soccer fans think the indoor game is a weak imitation of the "real game." Outdoor fans think indoor players are not as good, either. Of course, indoor fans think the outdoor game is too slow.

Some indoor players have gone on to outdoor stardom. Striker Predag Radosavljevik, known as Preki, played nine seasons in indoor leagues. He finished his indoor career with 399 goals and 384 assists. He joined MLS, in 1996, and was the 1997 MLS scoring champion with 41 points. He was also named the MLS MVP that season.

COLLEGE SOCCER

The first organized soccer match in the United States was a college men's game in 1869. Rutgers beat Princeton, 6–4. For about the next 100 years, college soccer was a loosely organized "club" sport. The first national college championship wasn't held until 1959. It was played by men's teams. The first women's championship wasn't held until 1982. What took so long? It was because colleges rarely sponsored sports teams for women until 1972, when Title IX was passed.

The college game now produces America's best soccer players. More than 900 colleges have soccer programs for men and women. Top male players go from colleges to Major League Soccer or to leagues in Europe. Top female players go on to the WUSA and some join the U.S. Women's National Team.

Universities such as Virginia, Indiana, and UCLA, for men, and North Carolina, Notre Dame, and Santa Clara, for women, are known for developing top players. More than 30 male and female players from the University of North Carolina have played for U.S. national teams. Successful college coaches can go on to lead the U.S. national teams, too. Steve Sampson of Santa Clara and Bruce Arena of the University of Virginia have coached the U.S. Men's National Team.

KYLE ROTE, JR.

Kyle Rote, Jr. was the most famous American soccer player in the 1970s. He was the son of football star Kyle Rote, Sr., who had been a receiver in the NFL for the New York Giants from 1951 to 1961. Kyle, Jr. was an all-state quarterback and defensive end in high school. He attended Oklahoma State University on a football scholarship and was following in his dad's footsteps. Then fate stepped in.

Kyle fell in love with soccer during a visit to England. When he returned to the United States, he switched to the University of the South, in Sewanee, Tennessee, where he could play soccer. He was team captain and MVP during each of his three seasons. He set a single-season school scoring record with 17 goals in only 12 games in 1971.

After he graduated, in 1972, Kyle was drafted by the Dallas Tornado of the pro North American Soccer League. The NASL was eager to attract fans, so the league promoted Kyle as the all–American boy who chose soccer over football. Kyle made a dramatic impact in 1973. He was the NASL's top scorer with 20 goals and 10 assists in 18 games. He won Rookie of the Year honors, and propelled the Tornado into the NASL championship game, which it lost to Philadelphia.

Kyle played in the NASL for seven seasons, and was chosen to play on the U.S. Men's National Team 15 times. He proved that players from American colleges could compete with the best players in the world.

LEGENDARY TEAM

UNC WOMEN'S TEAM

The University of North Carolina Tar Heels are one of the greatest dynasties in the history of college sports. They have won 17 national college soccer championships since 1981. Only three other colleges have won even one!

How's this for dominating a sport? The Tar Heels' record since 1979 is 487-22-11. They had records of 24-0-0, 25-0-0, 25-0-0, and 23-0-0 from 1990 through 1993. That's a total of 97 wins in a row! The Tar Heels won four straight national championships during that streak.

Why have the Tar Heels been so fabulously successful? In 1979, they became one of the first major colleges to field a women's soccer team. That allowed UNC to attract many of America's best female players. Many Tar Heels have won or shared national college player of the year awards: April Heinrichs (1986), Shannon Higgins (1988, 1989), Kristine Lilly (1990, 1991), Mia Hamm (1992, 1993), Tisha Venturini (1994), Debbie Keller (1996), Cindy Parlow (1997, 1998), Robin Confer (1997), and Lorrie Fair (1999).

The Tar Heels are coached by Anson Dorrance, who also coached the U.S. Women's National Team from 1986 through 1994 and led it to victory in the 1991 Women's World Cup. Nine of the 18 players on the 1991 World Cup championship team played for the Tar Heels! April Heinrichs is now the coach of the national team. Mia Hamm is, of course, one of its superstars.

NCAA CHAMPIONS

MEN'S CHAMPIONS (SINCE 1990)

The first championship was held in 1959

YEAR	CHAMPION	YEAR	CHAMPION
1990	UCLA	1996	St. John's
1991	Virginia	1997	UCLA
1992	Virginia	1998	Indiana
1993	Virginia	1999	Indiana
1994	Virginia	2000	Connecticut
1995	Wisconsin	2001	North Carolina

WOMEN'S CHAMPIONS

YEAR	CHAMPION	YEAR	CHAMPION
1982	North Carolina	1992	North Carolina
1983	North Carolina	1993	North Carolina
1984	North Carolina	1994	North Carolina
1985	George Mason	1995	Notre Dame
1986	North Carolina	1996	North Carolina
1987	North Carolina	1997	North Carolina
1988	North Carolina	1998	Florida
1989	North Carolina	1999	North Carolina
1990	North Carolina	2000	North Carolina
1991	North Carolina	2001	Santa Clara

>> THE WORLD GAME

THE TOP PRO LEAGUES

Soccer is the king of sports in more than 140 countries around the world. Wild crowds fill huge stadiums for games in Europe, Asia, South America, and Africa.

Many countries have leagues for professional clubs. These clubs often have a top–level team and several minor teams the way major league baseball teams have minor league teams to develop players. The best pro leagues are in four European countries: England, Germany, Italy, and Spain. Top players from around the world play in these leagues when they are not representing their own countries in regional championships or the World Cup.

Soccer in Europe is governed by the Union of European Football Associations (UEFA). The regular season lasts from August to May. The best teams play regular season league games and UEFA Champions League games during these months. The Champions League is made up of about 70 of the best clubs in Europe. The two best Champions League teams play for the European Cup.

Soccer players in Europe are given only a month to relax after the season. Training camp starts in July. But if it's a year when the World Cup or European Championships are to be held, then the players get no time off!

ENGLAND - PREMIERSHIP

The English Premier League, or Premiership, is one of the world's top club divisions. It is part of the professional English League, which has three other divisions that are not as good. The Premiership was called the English First Division when it was created in 1888.

There are 20 teams in the Premiership. Each team plays 38 league games during the regular season. The team with the best record receives the famous Premiership trophy as the Champions of England. Liverpool has won this title the most times (18), followed by Manchester United (12), Arsenal (11), and Everton (10).

FAST FACT

Striker Dixie Dean of Everton scored an amazing single-season record of 60 goals in 39 games during the 1927-28 First Division season. The Premiership record is 34 goals. Striker Alan Shearer of Blackburn had 34 in 40 games in 1994-95. Striker Andy Cole of Newcastle scored 34 in 40 games in 1993-94. Andy also scored a single-game Premiership record five goals for Manchester United, against Ipswich, in 1994-95.

LEGENDARY TEAM

The Manchester United Red Devils won five Premiership titles in the 1990's. In 1999, the Red Devils became the first English club to win three major titles in the same year. They won the Premiership trophy with a regular-season record of 22–13. Then they beat Newcastle, 2–0, to win the F.A. Cup. Then they took the European Cup by beating Germany's Bayern Munich, 2–1, in the UEFA Champions League final.

For good measure, the Red Devils also grabbed the Inter-Continental World Club Cup by beating Palmeiras of Brazil, 1–0. That made the Red Devils the club champions of the world.

That success has made Manchester United the most valuable sports team in the world. Red Devil jerseys and shorts are sold in many countries. The team is so popular that Rupert Murdoch offered to buy it for $1 billion in 1999 — and was turned down! Rupert had paid "only" $311 million for major league baseball's Los Angeles Dodgers in 1998.

Premiership teams also compete against England's other pro clubs for the English League Cup, and against England's pro and amateur teams for the Football Association (F.A.) Cup. The F.A. Cup is one of the world's oldest and most famous tournaments. It was first held in 1872.

The final F.A. Cup game is played each May at London's famous Wembley Stadium. Crowds of 80,000 fans wear the colors of their favorite team, wave team flags, and sing team songs to inspire their heroes to victory. Manchester United of the Premiership has won the F.A. Cup 10 times.

STAR TO WATCH DAVID BECKHAM

The most famous English soccer player is David Beckham of Manchester United. David is a true celebrity, with boyish good looks and a flashy lifestyle. Photographers are always chasing David, hoping to snap his picture for newspapers and magazines.

David is England's best attacking midfielder. He sets up goals with perfect passes. He has a wicked shot and is one of the best free-kick specialists in the world.

Born on May 2, 1975, near London, England, David achieved a childhood dream when he joined Manchester United in 1993. "I've been a United fan as long as I can remember," he says. "My bedroom wall used to be plastered with posters of United players."

David worked his way up to Manchester United's top team and was voted the Premiership's 1996–97 Young Player of the Year. He helped Manchester United win the English League title and the F.A. Cup that season. But his best was yet to come.

In 1998–99, David was one of the keys to United's "triple cup win" *(see box on page 83)*. He set up a bunch of goals for United's double-strike force of Andy Cole and Dwight Yorke, who together blasted 35 of the team's 80 Premiership goals that season.

Even though he's a superstar to English soccer fans, David says he's just one of the boys on the field. "There is a team-first spirit at Manchester United that has no equal," he says. "When you think of the number of stars

FAST FACT

The world's most important international soccer tournament for men — after the World Cup — is the UEFA European Championship. It is held every four years, between World Cup tournaments. The tournament features the best national teams in Europe. Euro '96 was held in England and won by Germany. Euro 2000 was held in Belgium and the Netherlands and won by France. Euro 2004 is scheduled to be played in Portugal.

we have at United, it's brilliant that no one is bigger than anyone else. We are all on the same level."

In 2001, a software company decided to bring David's high level of play into the homes of his many fans. A video game, *David Beckham Soccer*, was introduced revealing David's tips on passing, shooting, defending, and free kicks.

David continues to be one of the biggest names in English football.

ITALY - SERIE A

Italian kids dream of playing in Serie A and becoming stars like Roberto Baggio and Christian Vieri. The kids put posters of these superstars on their bedroom walls and hope to play in huge 85,000-seat stadiums like Milan's awesome San Siro.

AMAZING PLAYER

Sinisa Mihajlovic plays in defense for the Serie A team called Lazio. Sinisa was known as the "Bomber from Borovo" when he played in his native Yugoslavia from 1988 to 1991. Borovo, Yugoslavia is Sinisa's home town. He has an explosive shot and may be the best free-kick specialist in the world.

Sinisa is much like a baseball player whose team counts on him to pinch-hit home runs. He scored nine goals for Lazio in 1998-99, most of them from his free kicks. Sinisa claims that his shots have been clocked at nearly 100 miles per hour. But it took him years of practice to develop his power and accuracy. "As a kid, I used to practice kicking a ball against the garage door," he says. "Day after day, for hours on end, I made a terrible racket. The neighbors couldn't stand it!"

Serie A is Italy's top pro league. It is one of the oldest and toughest leagues in the world. Many of the greatest players from all over the world play pro soccer in Serie A, including Brazil's Ronaldo, France's Zinedine Zidane, Germany's Oliver Bierhoff, and Argentina's awesome Gabriel Batistuta.

Serie A was formed in 1898. It has 18 pro teams that play 34 matches apiece during the regular season, which lasts from late August until May. Top teams also compete in the UEFA Champions League. Serie A's best teams are Inter Milan, Juventus, AS Roma, Chievo, and Lazio Rome. Milan won its 16th Serie A championship in 1998–99. Milan has also won five European Cups. Juventus has won the most Serie A championships (25).

STAR TO WATCH CHRISTIAN VIERI

Christian Vieri is the world's most pricey soccer player. He is the first-string striker for Italy's national team and a big star for Inter Milan of Serie A. Inter Milan paid an eye-popping $50 million to acquire Christian from Lazio in 1999.

Can one soccer player really be worth $50 million? Christian is big, fast, and a great header of the ball. He creates chances for his teammates to score. His 11 goals during the 1998–99 season sent his former team, Lazio, to second place in Serie A and a berth in the Champions League. Christian was chosen as the best overall player and best Italian player of the Serie A season.

Inter Milan bought Christian because they wanted him to play alongside their other super-striker, Ronaldo. In his first game for Inter Milan, in 1999, Christian scored a hat trick (three goals) in a victory over Verona. He quickly became one of Serie A's best scorers.

Christian was born on July 12, 1973, in Bologna, Italy. He is the son of Roberto Vieri, a former Serie A player. Christian was raised in Australia after his family moved there, but he returned to Italy as a teenager to follow in his dad's footsteps.

Christian became one of the world's rising stars of soccer while playing for his dad's old club, Torino, from 1990 to 1993. Just like a top free agent in major league baseball, Christian was often acquired by the richest teams, who wanted to add him to their attack. He played for Pisa, Ravenna, Venice, and Atalanta before moving to Juventus in 1996–97.

Juventus qualified for the UEFA Champions League Cup in 1997, with Christian leading the way, but the team lost in the final game. Christian's scoring exploits caught the eye of Atletico Madrid, a club in the Spanish league. He was sold to Atletico Madrid for $16 million, and played for them in 1997–98. Then he came back to Italy to play for Lazio for one season, before he was sold to Inter for that record $50 million.

Toward the end of 2001, Christian thought about leaving Inter for another club. In March 2002, however, he changed his mind and extended his contract with the team through 2006. After firing 18 goals in only 17 games for Inter by April 2002, Christian continues to be worth every penny of his contract.

GERMANY - BUNDESLIGA

The players in Germany's Bundesliga really earn their pay. The Bundesliga is Germany's top pro league. It has 18 teams, each of which plays 32 games in the regular season. The top teams include Bayern Munich, Bayer Leverkusen, Hertha Berlin, Borussia Dortmund, Kaiserslautern, Wolfsburg, and Hamburg.

Bayern Munich is the country's most popular and successful team. The team's president is Franz Beckenbauer, Germany's legendary former World Cup and NASL star (see box on page 91).

Bayern Munich has won more Bundesliga championships (15) than any other team. Bayern Munich also won the

PREMIERSHIP CHAMPIONSHIPS (SINCE 1990)

1989-90	Liverpool	1995-96	Manchester United
1990-91	Arsenal	1996-97	Manchester United
1991-92	Leeds	1997-98	Arsenal
1992-93	Manchester United	1998-99	Manchester United
1993-94	Manchester United	1999-00	Manchester United
1994-95	Blackburn	2000-01	Manchester United

SERIE A CHAMPIONS (SINCE 1990)

1989-90	Naples	1995-96	Milan AC
1990-91	Sampdoria	1996-97	Juventus
1991-92	Milan AC	1997-98	Juventus
1992-93	Milan AC	1998-99	Milan AC
1993-94	Milan AC	1999-00	Lazio
1994-95	Juventus	2000-01	Roma

UEFA Cup in 1996. In 1998–99, the team set a Bundesliga record with 24 wins. They lost six games and had six ties.

Bayern's current stars are midfielder Steffan Effenberg, forward Carsten Jancker, and striker Giovane Elber. Superstar midfielder Lothar Matthaus left Bayern Munich to join the MetroStars of America's MLS for the 2000 season. Bayern Munich attracts crowds of almost 60,000 fans to their home games in Munich. When the team goes on the road, big crowds also show up.

Like other major European leagues, the Bundesliga's regular season ends in May. The team with the best record is the league champ. Then the champ really gets busy! Bayern Munich couldn't celebrate its 1999 championship for long because, in May, the team had to play in the German Cup final and the UEFA Champions League final.

In 2000, the once-feared German national team's reign ended. They managed to score only one point in the entire Euro 2000 tournament. The performance on the field was so poor that coach Erich Ribbeck announced his retirement the very next day, stating openly that the decision was a direct result of the team's "catastrophic elimination."

Rebuilding was a priority for the German team, and they qualified for the 2002 World Cup.

STAR TO WATCH   FRANKIE HEJDUK

Defender Frankie Hejduk of Bayer Leverkusen is Germany's favorite surfer dude.

Frankie was born in La Mesa, California, on August 5, 1974. He was a total beach bum as a kid. Frankie finished

LEGENDARY PLAYER

Franz Beckenbauer played defender and midfield for Bayern Munich from 1958 to 1977. He was nicknamed "The Kaiser," which means "the King" in German. Led by Kaiser Beckenbauer, Bayern Munich were the European Cup champs in 1974, 1975, and 1976. Franz was named European Player of the Year in 1972 and 1976. In 1977, he went to America to star in the North American Soccer League with the New York Cosmos *(see box on page 73).*

Franz played for Germany in three World Cup tournaments and in two World Cup finals. He was the captain of Germany's 1974 World Cup championship team. Later, he coached the team to the championship of the 1990 World Cup.

an impressive 10th in the National Junior High School Surfing Championship in 1988.

Frankie also loved to play soccer, and he has ridden a nice wave of success in that sport. He earned Under–16 All–America honors from the American Youth Soccer Organization in 1989. He attended college at UCLA, where he played for three years and earned second–team All–America honors from the Soccer Coaches Association in 1994.

Frankie was drafted by the Tampa Bay Mutiny of MLS in 1996. He joined the team late in the season and helped the Mutiny reach the semi–finals of the MLS playoffs. He scored a goal and had six assists in 23 games for the Mutiny in 1997.

Frankie has also been a member of the U.S. Men's National Team since 1996. He played for the United States at the 1996 Summer Olympics, and was one of the U.S. team's few bright spots in the 1998 World Cup tournament. The United States lost all three of its games, but Frankie's speed and peppy enthusiasm impressed scouts from Bayer Leverkusen. The team signed him to a three-year contract after the tournament.

Frankie joined Bayer Leverkusen late in the 1998–99 Bundesliga season. He showed why he is one of the most feared attacking defenders in all of soccer. Frankie creates panic among opposing defenders with his speed.

Frankie lives a fast-paced life, too. He plays for Bayer Leverkusen from fall to spring, and for the U.S. Men's

FAST FACT

Sometimes a coach's job isn't safe, even during a game. Tony Schumacher was fired as the head coach of Fortuna Cologne between halves of a 1999 Bundesliga match against Waldoff Mannheim! Fortuna was trailing, 2–0, at halftime. Team president Jean Loering was upset. He went into the dressing room and had a loud argument with Coach Schumacher, and fired him right then and there. An assistant coach took over in the second half, but he was unable to help the team avoid a very embarrassing 5–1 defeat.

BUNDESLIGA CHAMPIONS (SINCE 1990)

1989-90	Bayern Munich	1995-96	Borussia Dortmund
1990-91	Kaiserslautern	1996-97	Bayern Munich
1991-92	Stuttgart	1997-98	Kaiserslautern
1992-93	Werder Bremen	1998-99	Bayern Munich
1993-94	Bayern Munich	1999-00	Bayern Munich
1994-95	Borussia Dortmund	2000-01	Bayern Munich

National Team when he is needed. But he still finds time to surf. Frankie even asked his girlfriend Kim to marry him while he was surfing.

"It was in California," he says. "I had her in one hand and my board in the other. I got down on one knee and popped the question. I was waist deep in the water, and waves were crashing down on my head. It was cool."

Fans in Germany think Frankie is cool. They love his surfer looks, long hair, and tireless dashing about the field. He breaks into a funky reggae dance — shaking his hair and swinging his arms and legs back and forth — after he scores a goal.

This surfer dude rode quite a tough wave as he adjusted to life in Germany. He has been playing on the Third Division team for Bayer Levurkusen, which is not as good as its first team. Although he has not gotten much playing time professionally, he trained hard and participated in the World Cup 2002 for the U.S. team.

SPAIN - PRIMERA DIVISION

Spain's Primera Division has some of the best pro club teams — and most turbocharged fans — in all of Europe.

Spanish fans go bonkers for their favorite teams. About 110,000 fans regularly watch Barcelona play at the magnificent Nou Camp stadium. The team Real Madrid attracts 85,000 fans for its home games. Rayo Vallecano plays in front of about 6,000 fans in a small stadium. But Rayo fans work hard at being just as noisy as huge Real Madrid crowds. The Rayo fans blow horns, set off fireworks, and try to sing their team on to victory.

The Primera has 20 teams in all. Each team plays 35 games during the regular season. The team with the best regular-season record wins the Spanish League championship and earns a spot in the UEFA Champions League. All of Spain's pro teams may compete for the Spanish Cup.

The Primera's best teams are Valencia, Real Madrid, and Deportivo Coruna. Barcelona won the championship of the Spanish League for the 1997–98 and the 1998–99 seasons. Barcelona has won 16 league titles, the most in the history of the Primera Division. Valencia knocked off both Real Madrid and Barcelona on the way to winning the Spanish Cup championship in 1998–99. Deportivo Coruna took out Barcelona in the Spanish League championship of 1999–00. Real Madrid has been a powerhouse in European soccer, winning seven European Cups (as top team in the UEFA Champions League) and the 2000–01 Spanish League championship.

The Primera attracts superstars from other countries. Argentina's great Diego Maradona played for Barcelona from 1982 to 1984. Brazilian stars Romario and Ronaldo have also played in the league.

One of the hottest homegrown players is striker Raul Gonzalez Blanco. He is known by one name: Raul. In 1995, at age 17, Raul became the youngest player ever to play for Real Madrid. Still in his early twenties, he is a fan favorite with his good looks and electrifying goal–scoring.

STAR TO WATCH   KASEY KELLER

Kasey Keller grew up on an egg farm in Lacey, Washington. As a kid, he spent hours every day picking hundreds of eggs off a moving conveyor belt. Kasey's job was to choose the best eggs that had been laid by the farm's 25,000 chickens. Kasey had to be very careful not to crack the shells. "It was nonstop," he says. "Eggs would just keep coming at you."

Now soccer balls keep coming at Kasey. He is the goalkeeper for Tottenham Hotspur of the English

Premier League. He spent two seasons with Rayo Vallecano of Spain's Primera division. Rayo Vallecano was promoted from the second division to the Primera for the 1999–2000 season. The team was not expected to win many games, but Kasey gave Rayo Vallecano's fans something to cluck about. His *egg*–cellent goaltending was a big reason the team was roosting at the top of the standings after the first few weeks of the season.

Kasey has great reflexes and sees the action around him very well. He is calm and focused under extreme pressure. He never gets upset, even if things aren't going his way. You can trust Kasey to hold eggs and not break them.

Growing up on his parents' farm, Kasey learned to work hard. "He has given himself a tremendous work ethic," says his mother, Deter.

When Kasey wasn't picking eggs or baling hay, he was practicing and playing soccer. "He missed a lot of dances and social life in high school," says his mom. "But soccer was what he wanted to do."

By age 15, Kasey was so good that he was chosen to play for the U.S. Under–20 Men's National Team. He was very cocky when he accepted a soccer scholarship at the University of Portland in 1988. "The first year, everybody on campus thought he was big–headed," says Clive Charles, who was Kasey's coach at Portland.

As Kasey matured, his cockiness became a quiet confidence. He won college All–America honors as a senior. After graduating in 1991, he decided to play pro soccer

CURRENT STAR

in England. He spent five seasons with Millwall, a club team in a lower division. Kasey played well and was signed by Leicester City of the Premiership in 1996. Kasey shot to stardom by backstopping the team to victory in the 1997 English League Cup.

Kasey has also spent his fair share of time in goal for the U.S. National Team. He played at the 1996 Summer Olympics. He won the U.S. Soccer Male Athlete of the Year award in 1997, when he helped the U.S. men's team qualify for the 1998 World Cup tournament. Kasey posted six shutouts in nine qualifying matches! He was also U.S. Soccer's Male Athlete of the Year in 1999.

Kasey joined Spain's Primera for the 1999–2000 season. "Playing for Rayo Vallecano is definitely a challenge,"

PRIMERA DIVISION CHAMPIONS (SINCE 1990)

1989-90	Real Madrid	1995-96	Atletico de Madrid
1990-91	FC Barcelona	1996-97	Real Madrid
1991-92	FC Barcelona	1997-98	FC Barcelona
1992-93	FC Barcelona	1998-99	FC Barcelona
1993-94	FC Barcelona	1999-00	Deportivo Coruna
1994-95	Real Madrid	2000-01	Real Madrid

he says. "The same as it was when I joined England's Leicester City. That team had just won promotion to the Premiership. I hope at Rayo, I will have the same success."

Kasey returned to the U.S. National Team and continued to strive for success at the 2002 World Cup.

THE BEST OF THE REST
SOUTH AMERICA

South America is a hotbed of great soccer players. In many South American countries, kids play soccer at an early age and all year round on the fields, in the streets, or on the beaches. Great players such as Pelé, Diego Maradona, and Ronaldo began by playing soccer that way. The best young players are scouted and signed by local club teams and work their way up to a club's "first team," much like a baseball player rises through the minor leagues to the major leagues.

South American leagues are not as strong as European leagues. In Brazil and Argentina, many of the clubs need money, so they sell their best young players to rich clubs in Europe. Striker Ronaldinho, originally of the Brazilian club team Gremio, plays the 2002 season for French first division club Paris Saint–Germain. The star returned home to play with his national team, Brazil, for the 2002 World Cup.

SCOTLAND

Scotland's Premier Division is also one of the world's best leagues. It is dominated by two rival clubs in the city of Glasgow: Rangers and Celtic. Together, the two teams have won 20 of 24 championships since the league was formed in 1975. The Rangers won nine titles in a row from 1989 to 1997. Their streak was stopped by, you guessed it, Celtic.

Two–time U.S. Olympian and World Cup midfielder Claudio Reyna plays for Rangers. He played in Germany's Bundesliga from 1994 to 1999. He became the first American ever to captain a team in Europe when he led Wolfsburg in 1998. Claudio left the Bundesliga in 1999 to join Rangers. In 2001, Claudio made another move to the Sunderland Club of the English Premiership. He is captain of the United States Men's National Team and was a member of the 2002 U.S. World Cup team.

>> THE RULES OF THE GAME

Pelé called soccer "the beautiful game." It can also be called "the simple game." It is beautifully simple!

THE FIELD

Soccer is played on a rectangular field that must be between 100 and 130 yards long and between 50 and 100 yards wide. In international matches, such as the World Cup, the field must be at least 110 yards long and 70 yards wide. The field is divided by the *center line*. The *center circle* is where the teams kick off.

The lines on the side of the field are called *touchlines*, and the lines at either end are *goal lines*. The goals are 24 feet wide and 8 feet high. For a goal to count, the ball must cross the goal line and enter the net. The *goal area* is a 60-foot-by-18-foot rectangle in front of the net. Attacking players may not touch the goalie within this area unless the goalie has the ball and both of his feet are on the ground. The goal area is inside the *penalty area* — a 132-foot-by-54-foot rectangle. Inside the

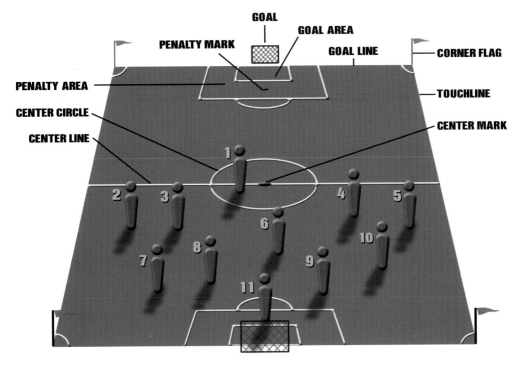

1 - STRIKER 2 - LEFT WING 3 - OFFENSIVE MIDFIELDER 4 - DEFENSIVE MIDFIELDER
5 - RIGHT WING 6 - WITHDRAWN STRIKER 7 - LEFT WING 8 - STOPPER 9 - SWEEPER
10 - RIGHT FULLBACK 11 - GOALKEEPER

penalty area, 12 yards from the goal line, is the *penalty mark*. This is the place from which players take penalty kicks. A quarter of a circle is in each corner of the field. These are where corner kicks (*see page 105*) are taken.

THE GAME

The game is played by two teams of 11 players each. There are two 45–minute periods. The team that scores more goals by kicking the ball into the other team's net is the winner.

Players may touch the ball with their head, chest, thighs, and feet. Only the goalie is allowed to use his hands. Players may use their hands on throw-ins, which take place after the ball has gone out-of-bounds.

Like American football, soccer begins with a coin toss. The winner may either kick off or choose an end of the field to defend. The kickoff is made from the center mark *(see diagram on previous page)*.

At kickoff, all players must be on their half of the field. The player who kicks off may not play the ball again until it has been touched by another player. After a score, the team that was scored upon kicks off from the center circle.

THE POSITIONS

Goalkeeper The goalie moves around the penalty area to stop shots from entering the net, or to take the ball away from attackers. After stopping a shot, the goalie starts an attack by kicking or throwing the ball to a teammate.

Defenders They are the last line of defense in front of the goalie. After a defender breaks up an opponent's play, he or she moves the ball to a midfielder to start an attack on the other team's goal. The defender who plays right in front of the goalkeeper is called the *sweeper*. The sweeper's job is to sweep the area clean of any offensive threat. The *stopper* is the defender who makes sure that the opposing team's striker doesn't score. The left and right *fullbacks*, or backs, are the defenders who play on the edges of the field.

Midfielders The four midfielders link the defense and the offense. They defend, move the ball, and score goals. The left and right *wings* play along the edges of the field. The *defensive midfielder* must be good at taking the ball from an opponent. The *offensive midfielder* is a playmaker who looks for scoring chances. The offensive midfielder usually has more chances to score goals than the defensive midfielder.

Forwards They score goals by attacking the other team's goal. The *striker* plays closest to the other team's goal. The *withdrawn striker* plays behind the striker and either passes the ball to the striker or shoots on his or her own.

STRATEGY

Soccer has almost no planned plays. Teams can't plan what to do because, from moment to moment, there will almost never be two situations that are alike. The only times that a team will try a play are on a free kick or a corner kick. On these two plays, defensive players must wait until the ball is put into play before they go after it. This gives the kicking team a head start.

Teams often have a playing *style*. For example, the famous Brazilian teams of the 1950s played with an *offensive style*. Brazil had many talented scorers, so they often sent four players to attack the opponent's goal. A team that has a *defensive style* will place most of its players in front of its own goal, to prevent scores. A defensive team's offense tries to catch attackers out of position and counterattack before the other team can recover.

Most teams play in a 4–4–2 formation with four defenders, four midfielders, and two strikers. The U.S. men's team sometimes uses a 3–5–2 formation, which has three central defenders, five midfielders, and two strikers. Two of the five midfielders are "flank" midfielders, who play defense and offense.

IMPORTANT RULES

Offside If a player without the ball is in his opponent's half of the field, at least two defenders, including the goalie, must be between him and the goal when the ball is passed to him. Otherwise, he is offside. If he is onside when the pass is attempted, he may receive it alone in front of the goalie.

Throw-in When the ball goes out–of–bounds, the team that didn't knock it out is given a throw–in. The ball must be thrown in, with both hands, from behind and above the player's head. The player's feet must be on the ground and outside, or on, the touchline. Goals may not be scored directly on a throw–in.

Goal Kick If the attacking team knocks the ball past the goal line and out–of–bounds, the defending team is awarded a goal kick. Goal kicks are taken from within the goal area and must travel beyond the penalty area. They may be taken by any player, but are usually taken by the goalkeeper.

Corner Kick If the defensive team knocks the ball past the goal line and out-of-bounds, the attacking team is awarded a corner kick from the corner spot. Goals are often scored on corner kicks. The player taking the corner kick sends the ball into the goal area, where most of the other players battle for it.

Free Kick *Indirect* free kicks are awarded after a player is offside or commits a minor violation, such as obstruction (blocking an opponent's path). *Direct* free kicks are awarded after major fouls, such as tripping. All free kicks are taken from the spot of the foul. The opposing team must stand at least 10 yards from the ball before it is kicked, unless the kick is within 10 yards of the goal. Then players may stand between the goalposts to defend. Goals may be scored right off a direct kick. Goals may not be scored off an indirect free kick until the ball has been touched by another player from either team.

Penalty Kick A penalty kick is awarded after a player commits a major foul in his team's penalty area. All players except the goalie and the player taking the kick must stand at least 10 yards away from the penalty spot, where the kick is taken. The goalie must stand on his goal line and not move forward until the ball is kicked. If the goalie stops the ball and it rebounds into the field, play continues. If the ball crosses the goal line on either side of the net (but doesn't go into the net for a goal), the attacking team is awarded a corner kick.

Shoot-Out Penalty kicks are used to decide games that are tied at the end of overtime. Each team takes five one-on-one penalty kicks against the goalie. The kicking players usually score, so one missed shot or a rare save by the goalie often makes the difference between victory and defeat.

THE OFFICIALS

Time is kept by the *referee*, who also enforces the rules. After a minor foul, the referee holds up a yellow warning card and awards a free kick. After a major foul, the referee holds up a red card and ejects the player from the game. The player's team may not use a substitute and must play shorthanded for the rest of the game. Two *assistant referees* help spot infractions and which team has knocked the ball out-of-bounds.

THE LINGO

Association Football the name for soccer in England in the late 1800s; shortened to *assoc*; later became *soccer*

Banana Kick putting spin on the ball while kicking it can make the shot curve like a banana around a wall of defenders

Bicycle Kick an acrobatic move in which a player is in mid-air with his back to the goal when he kicks the ball over his head into the goal; also called a *scissors* kick

Capped Players used to be given a cap to wear whenever they played for England's national team in an international match. This is no longer the case. A player who has appeared in 10 international matches for his country is now said to have "10 caps."

Card a colored card held up by the referee when a foul is committed; yellow signals a minor foul and red signals a major foul

Center to pass the ball into the penalty area from near a sideline

Cracker a booming shot into the net; also called a *scorcher* or a *thunderbolt*

Dribbling moving the ball with one's feet while running

Handball a rule violation that occurs when a player other than the goalie intentionally touches the ball with his hands or arms

Header using one's head to pass or direct the ball

Marking guarding an opponent

Screen to keep control of the ball while keeping one's body between the ball and a nearby opponent

Pitch the name for a soccer field in England

Trap when a player uses his feet, thighs, or chest to stop and control the ball

>> GLOSSARY

chaos a state of total confusion and disorder

chronic fatigue syndrome an illness that causes extreme weakness, muscle pain, and headaches

confederation a united or official group

founding member a person who helps to create and set up an organization

infraction when a rule is broken

political science the study of governments and politics

preliminary coming before the main part or item

rival a competitor of equal or almost equal ability

>> RESOURCES

BOOKS

Baddiel, Ivor. *Soccer*. New York, NY: DK Publishing, 1998.

Hamm, Mia, and Aaron Heifetz. *Go for the Goal: A Champion's Guide to Winning in Soccer and in Life*. New York, NY: HarperCollins, 2000.

Hornby, Hugh, and Andy Crawford. *Eyewitness: Soccer*. New York, NY: DK Publishing, 2000.

Longman, Jere. *The Girls of Summer: The U.S. Women's Soccer Team and How it Changed the World*. New York, NY: HarperCollins, 2001.

Macwilliam, Rab. *The World Encyclopedia of Soccer: A Complete Guide to the Beautiful Game*. New York, NY: Anness Publishing, Inc., 2001.

Stewart, Mark. *Soccer: A History of the World's Most Popular Game (The Watts History of Sports)*. New York, NY: Franklin Watts, Inc., 1998.

>> RESOURCES

MAGAZINES

SPORTS ILLUSTRATED FOR KIDS
135 West 50th Street
New York, NY 10020
(800) 992–0196
http://www.sikids.com

Soccer America
1235 10th Street
Berkeley, CA 94710
(510) 528–5000

WEB SITES

SPORTS ILLUSTRATED FOR KIDS
http://www.sikids.com
Check out the latest sports news, cool games,
and much more.

Fédération Internationale de Football Association
http://www.fifa.com
This site has up-to-the-minute news about soccer
all over the world.

>> RESOURCES

Major League Soccer
http://www.mlsnet.com
This is the official site of the MLS. You'll find news, stats, schedules, and links to each team Web site.

Women's United Soccer Association
http://www.wusa.com
This is the official site of the WUSA. You'll find news, stats, schedules, and links to each team Web site.

The National Soccer Hall of Fame
http://www.soccerhall.org
This site offers information about the National Soccer Hall of Fame, members of the Hall, and national soccer events. It has interactive games and a virtual tour of the museum.

>> INDEX